THE JOURNEY CONTINUES

Life's Travel Guide for Teens and Young Adults

Joan Garrett

With foreword by MARK SANBORN,

Author of the national bestseller *The Fred Factor*

iUniverse, Inc.

New York   Bloomington

The Journey Continues
Life's Travel Guide for Teens and Young Adults

iUniverse books may be ordered through booksellers or by contacting:

iUniverse
1663 Liberty Drive
Bloomington, IN 47403
www.iuniverse.com
1-800-Authors (1-800-288-4677)

ISBN: 978-1-4401-9653-9 (pbk)
ISBN: 978-1-4401-9654-6 (ebk)

Printed in the United States of America

iUniverse rev. date: 1/20/2010

Foreword

All great stories positively affect us. They can encourage our dreams and aspirations, speak to our fears or failings, and inspire us to become better. As we journey through life, we have the opportunity to be authors of our own very personal and unique stories.

Except for my upbringing and faith, no early life experience has done more to positively shape and influence me than serving as a state and national officer of the FFA. The FFA was the formative experience for me, and as the twig was bent, so grew the tree. Today I continue to work in leadership development as a speaker and author. I owe my current occupation to experiences and development provided me by the FFA.

In this book Joan Garrett presents twelve success principles that will help guide your life journey, and the quotes she has included can be used as inspiration for writing your own story. Make special note of the story examples that are included at the end of each chapter.

I hope that you won't just *read* this book, but will *use* it. Here's what I suggest.

Make notes and highlight as you go along. I have a deep respect for books, but my favorites are highlighted and underlined, so I can quickly go back to the best parts. Be an active reader.

Share your insights with family and friends. The value of a good idea is increased by sharing it. Look for lessons and insights you can share with others.

Write your own story. Think back to those important times in your life when you had an experience that truly mattered. Make some notes, and maybe even write the story out. One of the best parts of the legacy you leave your children and others is your story. Take Joan up on the invitation to contribute your own story for her next book.

And, of course, *thank others who have supported your journey.* Send a thank you note to a former teacher, pastor, parent, or friend who has made your journey better by his or her influence and example. And do whatever you can to encourage and support the development of the next generation of youth leaders.

Here is one of my stories. It is a simple story that taught me what leadership is all about.

It is not fair to ask of others what you are not willing to do yourself.

—Eleanor Roosevelt

When I was national FFA president and attended a chapter banquet, I made it a point to help however I could. Public speaking was, and still is, one of my favorite things to do, and that was my primary responsibility when a chapter invited me to their banquet. Thanks to my parents and FFA advisors through the years, I knew that what I did *before* and *after* I spoke was just as important—if not more so.

I arrived early for one chapter banquet while they were still setting up tables and chairs. I took off my valued blue and gold jacket and pitched in. At the end of the evening, the chapter advisor told me they had enjoyed my speech, but what he and his students remembered most wasn't the speech. It was that I had helped to set up chairs.

Mark Sanborn,
President, Sanborn & Associates, Inc.

Contents

About This Book

In a traditional sense, the notion of taking a journey focuses on getting from one place to another. Travel, especially long-distance trips, requires preparation and action, and success is determined by whether or not you arrive at a desired location. In this book, you will explore how the basic principles of travel relate to the ultimate journey—your life journey.

Your life journey doesn't primarily focus on ending up in a certain geographical location or achieving any particular measure of success. Its emphasis rests on all that happens between point A and point B—your birth and the end of your life. In his book *The Winners Manual for the Game of Life*, OSU head football coach Jim Tressel shares the following insight:

> Success is an everyday proposition. It isn't defined by a championship game or the day you get your diploma, get drafted by an NFL team, make the big sale, land the account of a lifetime, or get your law degree. Don't get me wrong; those are great days, and we should celebrate those accomplishments. But the key to a successful life is in the journey and the process. It's that emphasis on the journey to success that we work on each day, step by step…The thing we should most enjoy about any endeavor is the road we travel to get there.[1]

This book is designed to be used as a travel guide, and the information presented will help you focus on the road you take for your own personal journey. It is not meant to be a book that you read through once and never open again. Instead, it is suggested that the reader use this book much like an atlas and refer to it often.

It is best to travel at your own pace, so don't feel that you have to rush through this book. You may want to consider reading only one chapter a week and giving yourself plenty of time to reflect on what you have read before moving on. Take time to complete the personal reflection page at the end of each chapter.

You will find that each chapter concludes with two key sections. Following the summary page you will find a section titled "Words of Wisdom." It was former British Prime Minister Benjamin Disraeli who once said, "The wisdom of the wise and the experience of the ages are perpetuated by quotations." Over the years I have collected quotes from books, magazines, and the Internet, and I share numerous gems of great insight in each of these sections.

Most people, even those who aren't fond of reading, can appreciate an insightful person's ability to make a statement of great meaning and impact in just a few words. Search for the nuggets of wisdom that can positively influence your journey, but don't be overwhelmed by the number of quotations. Thirty have been selected, and they are numbered for a reason.

It is by design that this book has twelve chapters, just as there are twelve months in the year. After reading the book, begin again on the first day of a month and reread each of the "Words of Wisdom" sections. Use the numbering system to keep you on track, while you read and reflect upon one quote each day of the month, thus giving yourself a daily source of motivation and inspiration for an entire year. Referring back to your travel guide each day will help to reinforce the principles of success that you will be learning more about.

Another key section at the end of each chapter is titled "A Lesson from a Story." In the first chapter you will learn that my inspiration for writing this book came as a result of attending the 2007 national FFA convention in Indianapolis. In recognition of that source of inspiration, I have invited FFA members to share personal stories that provide examples of how a quote's key message has been realized in their own lives.

For readers not familiar with FFA, the organization is recognized as the premier agricultural education student youth organization in the nation. Once known as the Future Farmers of American, the organization changed its name in 1988 to the National FFA Organization in order to reflect the expanding career field of agricultural education. Founded in 1928, the organization now has a membership that exceeds 507,000, with over 7,400 local chapters found in all fifty states, Puerto Rico, and the Virgin Islands.

Being a member of the FFA, however, is not a prerequisite for learning from this book. Chances are that, as a young adult interested in leadership and personal development, you have benefited from membership in some type of youth organization. Maybe you excelled in a sports program, participated in an honor society or student government, or were involved in a church-sponsored youth program. Were you a member of DECA, FCCLA, 4-H, Boy Scouts, Girl Scouts, drama club, debate team, Mock Trial, science club, band, choir, yearbook staff, technology club, or another organization? Regardless of your organization affiliation, you will be able to relate each story to *your* personal experiences when you answer the question at the end of each story. Challenge yourself to read the stories and reflect on your own examples.

Now, let the journey continue ...

Chapter 1

Selecting the Next Destination

Setting Goals to Get There

People with goals succeed because they know where they're going.

—Earl Nightingale

When I was a teenager growing up in rural Ohio, in the early 1980s, my personal and leadership development was greatly influenced by involvement in student organizations. FFA, FHA/HERO (now known as FCCLA), and 4-H activities created a busy schedule, but I thrived in youth programs that provided opportunities for me to develop leadership, parliamentary procedure, and public-speaking skills.

Despite being a four-year FFA member from 1979–1983, I did not attend my first national FFA convention until 2007. My son, Clay, was selected to participate in the national FFA band, and I made the trip to Indianapolis for my first national convention experience so that I could hear him perform. The inspiration for this book came as a result of attending that convention.

While attending the general sessions, I heard several of the retiring addresses given by national officers. What an exciting journey they shared! But even though the national officers' FFA experiences were ending, those young leaders seemed to understand what John Dewey meant when he said, "Arriving at one goal is the starting point to another." As an American educational reformer, philosopher, and psychologist, Dewey recognized that new experiences and challenges are always on the horizon, and each person's journey is meant to continue rather than end prematurely.

If there is one concept in which the experts on human achievement agree, it would be the importance of setting goals. Success at school, at work, or in our personal lives does not happen by accident. It happens by design, through intentional planning and hard work. The process goes like this: a dream becomes a goal, a goal requires action, and the action results in success and fulfillment. Establishing goals and working to achieve them helps you to reach your individual potential. You become more confident about envisioning endless possibilities and making them your reality.

An underlying belief that should guide our lives is this: the quest for success is actually a journey. Arriving at a particular place or achieving a certain goal doesn't mean you are finished. There is much more of life to experience. You can't afford to become complacent and satisfied with resting on your laurels, because if you do your journey will come to a grinding halt. It's like hitting the pause button on the DVD player. You are left hanging and wondering what comes next.

That is why it is crucial for you to continually establish goals for the personal, family, and professional parts of your life. In many ways, a goal acts as a compass, telling you which direction you should travel. If you move in any direction other than toward your goals, you will miss out on the opportunities and experiences necessary for achieving success.

THE VALUE OF SETTING GOALS

Living without goals is like taking a trip without having first chosen a destination. If you do not know where you are going, you probably will not get very far from home. The real dilemma is whether you are going to select a destination and establish a path to reach it, or allow yourself to be swept along with the tide, letting others such as your family, friends, and colleagues determine where you will end up. The choice is entirely up to you. A productive and fulfilling journey will not take care of itself; it is your responsibility to plan it yourself. If you were to just start driving, you would have no clue where you will end up. But when you plan ahead and know where you are going, you can successfully make the journey and enjoy your experiences along the way. Goals enrich your life in numerous ways by providing the following.

- *Direction*: Goals outline a path toward your destination.
- *Enjoyment*: Pursuing goals can make your life more fun, more interesting, and more challenging.
- *Independence*: Goals help you take charge and choose your own path for your life.
- *Motivation*: Setting goals gives you a reason to get moving and take action.

- *Network*: While working to achieve goals, you will have many opportunities to meet new people, thus expanding your personal and professional contacts.
- *Purpose*: Goals provide a sense of meaning and a reason to start really living. Goals help you reach your potential and realize fulfillment.

CREATE *SMART* GOALS

One of the first leadership lessons I learned as a teen focused on the concept of developing *SMART* goals. Each letter in the acronym identifies a key principle for ensuring that a goal is achievable. The criteria for *SMART* goals are outlined below.

Specific: The first key to making a goal obtainable is to make it specific. Think about what would happen if you went into the paint department of a home improvement store and told the sales person, "I would like some paint." Without identifying the specifics of color, type of gloss, interior or exterior use, price range, and even brand name, there is no telling what you would get. The same is true for setting goals. You have to spell out what you intend to do. You cannot accomplish a goal if you cannot articulate it in specific terms.

Measurable: Goals must be measurable. Numbers or amounts included as part of a goal help to quantify the desired outcome. This component of measurement reduces ambiguity and helps to assess progress in achieving the desired end result. State your goal as objectively as possible, so that you will be able to answer the question, "Have I achieved this goal?" with a simple yes or no answer. Without criteria for measurement, you don't really have a goal; it is just a good idea.

Action oriented: Goals are only realized when the gap between intentions and actions is removed. Both planning and action are crucial. Napoleon Hill, one of America's earliest authors of personal-success literature, once said, "It's not what you are going to do, but it's what you are doing now that counts."

Realistic: While dreams may be considered fantasy, goals must be grounded and realistic. So start by honestly examining yourself. Consider your interests, experiences, education, personal strengths and weaknesses, and material/financial resources. Ask yourself, "Do I have what it takes to achieve this goal?"

Time-Sensitive: All goals need deadlines. Most goals never go from dream to reality unless there is some kind of deadline. When you set a goal, establish a completion date. Deadlines can be great motivators, and they can encompass both short- and long-term time intervals. One goal may be realized in as little as a week or a month, while another goal may take years or even decades for you to successfully reach.

CATEGORIZE AND BALANCE YOUR GOALS

One of the keys to experiencing a successful journey throughout life is to maintain a sense of balance. Setting goals for only one area of your life tends to put blinders on you and makes your focus too narrow. The best way to avoid this pitfall is to divide your goals into categories that will enable you to keep perspective and bring balance to your goals. Common goal categories include:

- Family
- Spiritual/faith
- Friendships/significant relationships
- Athletic/fitness
- Educational
- Personal growth
- Career
- Financial: income/retirement
- Recreational activities
- Travel
- Hobbies/things you want to learn to do
- Things you want to acquire

WRITE, REVIEW, AND REVISE GOALS REGULARLY

One of the most productive things you can do is to spend some time in reflection, thinking and writing out your list of goals. The act of writing your goals begins a process that enables you to make a commitment to yourself. Seeing goals on paper is the first step of turning them into reality. When goals are set, you subconsciously set your mind in motion to work day and night to come up with ways to achieve them. Zig Ziglar, one of America's top motivators, once said, "A goal properly set is halfway reached." There is no better way to set a goal than to get it down on paper.

Do you ever make "to do'" lists for daily or weekly tasks? Have you found that the more you look at that list, the more things you are able to accomplish? That is why you usually keep those kinds of lists visible by posting them on the refrigerator or bulletin board, sticking them on your calendar, or entering them into an electronic planner. It works the same way with goals. You need to review your goal list often, at least once a week. Regularly reviewing your goals helps motivate you to work and move in the direction required for their completion. It helps you focus on the destination.

After participating in the Christian Walk to Emmaus program several years ago, I established a journal-writing tradition that I complete each

December between Christmas and New Year's Eve. In a journal that I have designated for each of my sons, I write a letter that summarizes each of their challenges, accomplishments, and experiences for the year. In my own personal journal, I list the most memorable events and experiences of the year, and I include a list of goals to accomplish during the next year.

When I sit down to write, I begin by reviewing the list for the year that is ending. Taking time for reflection is essential for keeping me on track. As I bring closure to the year, it gives me great pleasure to check off the goals that were achieved. Some goals will still be in progress and will be carried over to the next year, while other goals have been revised and accomplished along the way. There have even been a few instances when I have lost interest in a goal and crossed it off the list. Goal-setting is an ongoing process, and it is beneficial to look back and assess how you have added or changed goals along the journey. Goals are not carved in stone—there is no rule that says you can't change them.

SUMMING IT UP

Key points from this chapter include:

- A dream becomes a goal, a goal requires action, and the action results in success or achievement.

- A goal acts as a compass, telling you which direction you should travel.

- Goals enrich your life by providing direction, enjoyment, independence, motivation, and purpose.

- It is important to establish SMART goals that are **S**pecific, **M**easurable, **A**ction oriented, **R**ealistic, and **T**ime sensitive.

- The act of writing your goals helps to establish a personal commitment to seeing them achieved.

- You should avoid being too narrowly focused by setting goals that cover a wide variety of categories, in order to maintain perspective and balance in your life.

- It is a good idea to write, review, and revise goals regularly.

Oliver Wendell Holmes, an American physician, professor, and author who was regarded by his peers as one of the best writers of the nineteenth century, once said, "The great thing in this world is not so much where we are but in what direction we are moving." Remember, you can work toward achieving your goals no matter where you are today. Now is the time to select your next destination.

WORDS OF WISDOM

1. Your goals are the road maps that guide you and show you what is possible for your life.

    —Les Brown

2. Setting goals is the first step in turning the invisible into the visible.

    —Tony Robbins

3. Goals are not only absolutely necessary to motivate us. They are essential to really keep us alive.

    —Robert H. Schuller

4. In the long run, men hit only what they aim at. Therefore, they had better aim at something high.

    —Henry David Thoreau

5. A dream doesn't become reality through magic; it takes sweat, determination, and hard work.

    —Colin Powell

6.   How do you go from where you are to where you wanna be? I think you have to have an enthusiasm for life. You have to have a dream, a goal. And you have to be willing to work for it.

—Jim Valvano

7.   A goal is a dream with a deadline.

—Napoleon Hill

8.   If you want to reach a goal, you must "see the reaching" in your own mind before you actually arrive at your goal.

—Zig Ziglar

9.   People with clear written goals accomplish far more in a shorter period of time than people without them could ever imagine.

—Brian Tracy

10.   Written goals have a way of transforming wishes into wants, can'ts into cans, dreams into plans, and plans into reality. Don't just think it—ink it!

—Dan Zadra

11.   Goals give us somewhere to set our sights. Goals are like target practice—we get ready, we aim for what we want, and we fire away!

—Debbie Macomber

12.   All your dreams can come true if you have the courage to pursue them.

—Walt Disney

13.   Many people fail in life, not for lack of ability or brains or even courage, but simply because they have never organized their energies around a goal.

—Elbert Hubbard

14.   Make no small plans, for they have no power to stir the soul.

—Niccolo Machiavelli

15.   All successful people have a goal. No one can get anywhere unless he knows where he wants to go and what he wants to be or do.

—Norman Vincent Peale

16.   If you set goals and go after them with all the determination you can muster, your gifts will take you places that will amaze you.

—Les Brown

17.   All who have accomplished great things have had a great aim, have fixed their gaze on a goal which was high, one which sometimes seemed impossible.

—Orison Swett Marden

18.   Goals allow you to control the direction of change in your favor.

—Brian Tracy

19.   Just as soon as you attain to one ambition you see another one glittering higher up still. It does make life so interesting.

—Anne Shirley

20.   When we focus our thoughts on a specific goal, something wonderful and magical occurs. Our minds start churning, finding ways to help us achieve our dreams.

—Debbie Macomber

21.   If you are bored with life, if you don't get up every morning with a burning desire to do things—you don't have enough goals.

—Lou Holtz

22.   We must begin with the end in mind.

—Stephen Covey

23.   To achieve a big goal, you are going to have to become a bigger person. You are going to have to develop new skills, new attitudes, and new capabilities. You are going to have to stretch yourself, and in so doing, you will be stretched forever.

—Jack Canfield

24.   Decide what you want, decide what you are willing to exchange for it, establish your priorities, and go to work!

—H. Lamar Hunt

25.   Goals help you channel your energy into action.

—Les Brown

26.   The greater danger for most of us lies not in setting our aim too high and falling short, but in setting our aim too low, and achieving our mark.

—Michelangelo Buonarroti

27.   The key lesson is that anyone with the ambition, properly channeled and focused, has the potential to achieve more than anyone would have imagined.

—John Wooden

28.   By focusing on our goals, we stay centered on what's important and are better able to sort out the distractions that try to slow us down.

—Debbie Macomber

29.   We all have dreams. But in order to make dreams into reality, it takes an awful lot of determination, dedication, self-discipline, and effort.

—Jesse Owens

30.   Whatever the mind of man can conceive and believe, it can achieve.

—Napoleon Hill

A LESSON FROM A STORY

There are three types of people in this world: Those who make things happen, those who watch things happen, and those who wonder what happened. We all have a choice. You can decide which type of person you want to be. I have always chosen to be in the first group.

—Mary Kay Ash

I attended a small rural school; there were fifty-three students in my graduating class. Our agriculture education program was small as well, and not very popular. I joined FFA my freshman year (1999) and was really excited—until I attended class on the first day of school. As I sat there, in a room full of boys, I kept waiting for other girls from the freshman class to come in … they never came. So, there I was, the only girl, surrounded by boys, and judging by the looks they were giving me, I knew I wasn't the only one wondering what in the world I was doing there.

My parents encouraged me to put my best foot forward and show those boys a thing or two, so I decided to stick it out. We started the year by learning about the FFA and the numerous opportunities it provided for its members. I became extra interested in the four degrees members could earn: Greenhand, Chapter, State, and American. Our advisor told us that no one had received their state degree since 1993, and there had not been an American Degree recipient since he had been an advisor at the school. I knew at that moment that I was going to earn those prestigious awards.

I received a lot of scrutiny from my classmates and even some of my family members; they said that with a supervised agricultural experience of only dairy goats, I was never going to make it. At that point, I knew that if they weren't going to help me make it happen, I was going to have to do it on my own.

On May 5, 2001, I crossed the stage at the Ohio State FFA Convention, State FFA Degree in hand, and then again at the National FFA Convention on October 30, 2004, with my American FFA Degree proudly in hand. Both times I made my way across the stage beaming with pride at my accomplishments, and both times I came off the stage sobbing into the arms of family and friends, because I had finally accomplished what few people thought was possible.

I'm proud to say that a couple years after I joined, the West Unity FFA chapter became quite popular with the girls of Hilltop High School, and I feel that I, in some small way, paved the way for those girls who are passing through the program and keep providing my home chapter with a small, but noteworthy, supply of State and American FFA Degree winners.

I learned that only I can make my dreams happen and also that the decisions I make today could possibly affect the accomplishments of others down the road. This is a lesson we can all reflect upon, and now, as a teacher of agriculture and FFA advisor, I try to encourage my students to make their dreams happen—as my advisor encouraged me to accomplish mine.

Jessica (Short) Tracey,
Millcreek-West Unity FFA, Class of 2002
Plymouth FFA Advisor

Set high goals. What have you accomplished that others said couldn't be done?

PERSONAL REFLECTIONS

Write your favorite quote from this chapter in the space below:

_____
_____
_____
_____
_____
_____
_____

Why is this quote especially meaningful to you?

_____
_____
_____
_____
_____
_____
_____
_____
_____

Practice writing a goal statement below.

_____
_____
_____
_____
_____
_____
_____
_____

Which of the following "SMART" criteria are included in your goal?

_____ Specific
_____ Measurable
_____ Action oriented
_____ Realistic
_____ Time-specific

Chapter 2

Focusing on the Road

Having Rules to Guide You

Standing in the middle of the road is very dangerous; you get knocked down by the traffic from both sides.

—Margaret Thatcher

Valuable time spent setting goals will guide your way to the next destination. Let's say, for example, that you and your family will be driving to Denver, Colorado, for a snow-skiing vacation over the New Year's holiday. With that goal established, you are faced with the basic necessity of understanding driving laws, knowing how to operate a vehicle, and having the experience to know how the vehicle will handle road surfaces negatively impacted by rainy, snowy, and icy weather conditions. Lacking this knowledge will negatively impact your ability to successfully make the trip.

The opening quote from Margaret Thatcher tells us that a person standing in the middle of the road is in a very precarious position. Likewise, as you make your personal success journey, you definitely do not want to find yourself standing in the middle of the road. The easiest way to avoid such a predicament is to have a clear understanding of your core values. When you have strong values and beliefs, you have an anchor to hold you steady, even when the weather gets rough. You also have a built-in compass that is always a dependable guide. Values and beliefs are the rules that guide you as you experience life.

LIFE IS SIMPLER WHEN WE KNOW WHAT WE VALUE

As a new parent, I read a lot of material on the topic of disciplining children. Discipline is often defined as training that instructs, molds, strengthens or perfects. During the early years, parents establish and reinforce fundamental truths or rules to children as a way of guiding behavior. When my sons were young, we practiced reciting "the five rules of life" as part of a bedtime routine. I'm not sure why I chose five, but maybe it was because you can easily count to five using one hand. Our five rules included:

1. Have faith in God.
2. Be good.
3. Get along with others.
4. Work hard and play hard.
5. Make something of your life.

What made these "rules" meaningful was grounding them in my own personal values. Even though parents may make every effort to instill values in their children, the ultimate acceptance of them and the decision to live by them rests with each individual. Without clear values as a guide, you will tend to wander around, bouncing from one thing to another like a pinball in an arcade game, trying to discover who you are. Knowing your values helps you to:

*   follow a clear set of rules and guidelines for your actions.
*   make good decisions and set priorities for how to use your resources, such as time, money, and talents.
*   fill your life with the people, places, and things that support your ideals while challenging you to grow.
*   live with integrity. The more you live true to your values, the more fulfilled and peaceful you will be.

What do you value? What qualities are truly important to you? What priorities determine your actions? Brainstorm a personal list of values in answer to those questions. Include every admirable character quality you consider to be important. Just as the alphabet is fundamental in learning to read, the ABC approach may be helpful in generating your list of personal values. Here are ideas to get you started:

A: Achievement, Adventure, Appreciation
B: Balance, Belief in Yourself, Belonging
C: Cooperation, Commitment, Compassion
D: Determination, Dedication, Discipline
E: Education, Effort, Endurance
F: Faith, Family, Freedom

G: Goals, Generosity, Guidance
H: Health, Honesty, Hope
I: Integrity, Intelligence, Ingenuity
J: Justice, Joy, Job
K: Kindness, Knowledge, Keenness
L: Love, Laughter, Loyalty
M: Money, Moderation, Making a Difference
N: Nature, Neatness, Nerve
O: Order, Optimism, Opportunity
P: Peace, Patience, Perseverance,
Q: Quality, Quietude, Quickness
R: Relationships, Religion, Respect
S: Significance, Sincerity, Service
T: Time, Talent, Truthfulness
U: Unity, Uniqueness, Usefulness
V: Vision, Victory, Vitality
W: Work, Will Power, Wisdom
X: eXcellence, eXcitement, eXperience,
Y: Youthfulness, Yearnings, Yields
Z: Zaniness, Zest, Zeal

It is important to narrow your list down and make it more manageable. A list that is too long becomes overwhelming. There is no established rule for how long your list should be, but a list in the range of ten to fifteen values would be very meaningful. If you have more, consider cutting out the ones that just barely made your list, or combine multiple values that are nearly identical, like when you combine truthfulness and honesty, commitment and dedication, or determination and perseverance.

The next step is to prioritize your list. This is usually the most time consuming and difficult step, because it requires some intense thinking. Begin by asking yourself these questions: Which of these values is truly the most important to me in life? If I could only satisfy one of these values, which one would it be? The answer to this question is your number-one value. Then move down the list and ask which remaining value is the next most important to you, and so on, until you've sorted the whole list in priority order.

So let's say that someone has sorted their list and came up with the following:

- Love
- Relationships
- Loyalty
- Peace
- Comfort
- Happiness
- Hobbies
- Fitness/Health

- Education
- Adventure
- Financial gain
- Achievement

What does this list say about a person? When you know the hierarchy of a person's values, you can generally predict his or her behavior. If they live true to their values, they will lead a life focused on love, relationships, and loyalty above all else. Family and friendships will be extremely important, and this individual is unlikely to put career success above family.

On the other hand, let's say another person prioritized their values in exactly the opposite order:

- Achievement
- Financial Gain
- Adventure
- Education
- Fitness/Health
- Hobbies
- Happiness
- Comfort
- Peace
- Loyalty
- Relationships
- Love

What do you know about this person? Now we have someone who is probably very career oriented. They will lead a very different life when compared to the person who holds love as his or her top value. Succeeding and becoming wealthy is more important to this person than personal relationships, so, if he or she had a choice between advancing their career or going on a family vacation, he or she would almost always put career first.

Is one list right and one list wrong? No. Values are deeply held personal beliefs, and it is very unlikely that any two lists are exactly the same. It is not an easy task to put a list in rank order, but by consciously prioritizing your values you'll be able to rely on them when you need to make an important decision in the future.

Once you have your list narrowed down and prioritized, keep it in a place where that you can read it daily. Set it on the bedside table by your alarm clock, tape it on the bathroom mirror, or post it on the refrigerator. Think about your values often, and focus on what they mean to you. Remember, a successful life journey is based on making decisions and choices that hold true to your values.

LIVING OUT YOUR VALUES:
THE POWER OF SELF-DISCIPLINE

Managing your life according to your values is not always easy. You can expect to have your values tested daily by those who do not share them. Negative people may mock you when you display a positive attitude, and people who don't have extended families living nearby may not understand your devotion to family. Another test comes from those whose priorities are different from your own. They may attempt to persuade you to adopt theirs or to make unwise compromises.

Living true to your values and beliefs requires implementing a plan for achieving success, committing yourself to it, and then following through. Recognize that nothing worthwhile ever comes easily or without a price. It is wise to be willing to give up some temporary enjoyment in order to work at something that has a more lasting reward. Success comes when you pay now and play later. Self-discipline calls for a measure of delayed gratification, the willingness and the ability to postpone enjoyment now so that you can experience gain in the future. It means the work, the pain, and the sacrifice comes now, and the rewards come later.

People sometimes get into trouble when their values and their feelings collide. When your values determine you should take an action that will hurt you or cost you something, it can be harder to follow through. For example, if one of your values is integrity, and you saw a person drop a fifty-dollar bill on the ground, you probably wouldn't have a difficult time in calling out to a person and returning the money.

But what if you see your supervisor stealing from the company where you work, and you knew that reporting the incident might get you fired? That choice could be more difficult, especially if you knew that losing your job would result in loss of income and health insurance for your family. But your values, not your feelings, should influence your actions and decisions.

By choosing to live by your values every day, you choose the higher road in life. You may not always *get* what you desire, but you will always *be* the kind of person you desire to be. It is wise to consider the differences in the outcomes for people who make their life's journey with and without values to guide them.

A person *without* guiding values:	A person *with* guiding values:
Words and actions do not align	Words and actions agree
Influenced by moods	Guided by values
Does what is easiest	Does what is right
Gives excuses	Looks for solutions
Quits when challenged	Perseveres when challenged
Depends on external motivation	Relies on internal motivation
Choices lead to failure	Choices contribute to success

REALIGNING YOUR VALUES

Establishing your list of values is not a once-in-a-lifetime task. Your values are a compass for where you are at this point in your life, but, as your destination changes, you will find that your compass will help you realign your journey. If you continue living according to the same set of values, then you can expect to get similar results to what you are already experiencing.

Chances are a time will come when you need to make changes. You may be asking yourself lots of questions at this point in your life. What is my ideal dream job? How can I make a difference in my community? Will I ever get married? Who will be my spouse? How many children should I have? When will I be financially able to retire? Will I ever travel and see different parts of the world?

How can one or more of these questions become a positive reality for you? The answer is: by realigning your values. By revising your list of values and consciously acting with that list in mind, you can change your behavior and therefore your results. For example, let's say your top value has been health and wellness. As a result, you are very diet conscious and you are committed to exercise and recreational activities that contribute to your fitness goals. You are now at an ideal weight and in great physical condition.

But what would happen if you changed your top value to education? You might find yourself cutting back on exercise for a time and investing more energy into education and training that will prepare you for the dream job you have always wanted. Your investment in health and wellness may slide a little in the short term, but because it may still remain one of your top values it won't be completely forgotten. It just isn't number one anymore. So now, by focusing intently on the new top value of education, you eventually succeed in landing that dream job.

Eventually you might become content in your dream job and decide to shift your top value to service, because you want to give back to others by volunteering for a nonprofit organization. Through this process of consciously shifting your values, your focus has changed: from health/wellness to education to career to service. If you had maintained only the original list of values, you might never have experienced other opportunities for personal growth and development.

When you are reassessing values, repeat the process of listing and prioritizing, but this time keep in mind the goals you want to pursue on your success journey. Start by considering your top ten to fifteen goals. More than a hundred is even okay; it will just take longer to prioritize your list. You will soon realize that one list of values may not provide enough direction to help you achieve all your goals. At each point of success, it's a good time to realign your values list while considering the next goal on your list.

This chapter's opening quote from Margaret Thatcher provides an analogy for the importance of following your values as you strive to achieve your goals. Read it once more. "Standing in the middle of the road is very dangerous; you get knocked down by the traffic from both sides." Knowing and following your values helps you assess situations and see the positive and negative or right and wrong of a situation.

Standing in the middle of the road puts you in a very dangerous gray area. If you stay there too long you *are* likely to get knocked down by traffic coming from both directions. Choose a lane now, get out of the middle, and rely on your values to be the rules for the road, as you continue the journey.

SUMMING IT UP

Key points from this chapter:

- Your values are strong personal beliefs, which guide your behavior and influence the decisions you make regarding how you live your life.

- Values provide you with an anchor and compass as you continue the success journey.

- It is advisable to review your prioritized list of ten to fifteen values daily.

- You can expect to have your values tested daily by those who do not share them. Self-discipline and the willingness to delay gratification will help keep you on track.

- Our values, not our feelings, need to control our actions and decisions.

- Establishing your list of values is not a once-in-a-lifetime task. Frequently reexamine your list, and realign it with current goals.

Mahatma Gandhi once said, "Your beliefs become your thoughts. Your thoughts become your words. Your words become your actions. Your actions become your habits. Your habits become your values. Your values become your destiny." Choose your values with great care.

WORDS OF WISDOM

1.   Real integrity is doing the right thing, knowing that nobody's going to know whether you did it or not.

                                                           —Oprah Winfrey

2.   It was character that got us out of bed, commitment that moved us into action, and discipline that enabled us to follow through.

                                                           —Zig Ziglar

3.   If you set out to be liked, you would be prepared to compromise on anything at any time, and you would achieve nothing.

                                                           —Margaret Thatcher

4.   Accept responsibility for your life. Know that it is you who will get you where you want to go, no one else.

                                                           —Les Brown

5.   Nothing shapes your life more than the commitments you choose to make ... We become whatever we are committed to.

                                                           —Rick Warren

6.   Listening to your heart is not simple. Finding out who you are is not simple. It takes a lot of hard work and courage to get to know who you are and what you want.

—Sue Bender

7.   Building healthy self-esteem requires integrity. This means honesty—matching who you are on the inside with who you are on the outside.

—Fran Hewitt

8.   Don't compromise yourself. You are all you've got.

—Janis Joplin

9.   Be more concerned with your character than your reputation, because your character is what you really are, while your reputation is merely what others think you are.

—John Wooden

10.   It is our choices that show what we truly are, far more than our abilities.

—J. K. Rowling

11.   You must take personal responsibility. You cannot change the circumstances, the seasons, or the wind, but you can change yourself.

—Jim Rohn

12.   In the long run, we shape our lives, and we shape ourselves. The process never ends until we die. And the choices we make are ultimately our own responsibility.

—Eleanor Roosevelt

13.   What you have outside you counts less than what you have inside you.

—B. C. Forbes

14.   If a man does not keep pace with his companions, perhaps it is because he hears a different drummer. Let him step to the music which he hears, however measured or far away.

—Henry David Thoreau

15.   Remember that what's right isn't always popular, and what's popular isn't always right.

—H. Jackson Brown, Jr.

16.   Just as your car runs more smoothly and requires less energy to go faster and farther when the wheels are in perfect alignment, you perform better when your thoughts, feelings, emotions, goals, and values are in balance.

—Brian Tracy

17.   What you are will show in what you do.

—Thomas Edison

18.   The easiest thing to be in the world is you. The most difficult thing to be is what other people want you to be. Don't let them put you in that position.

—Leo Buscaglia

19.   This above all: to thine own self be true. And it must follow, as the night the day, thou canst not then be false to any man.

—William Shakespeare

20.   Reputation is what others perceive you as being, and their opinion may be right or wrong. Character, however, is what you really are, and nobody truly knows that but you. But you are what matters most.

—John Wooden

21.   A reputation, once broken, may possibly be repaired, but the world will always keep their eyes on the spot where the crack was.

—Joseph Hall

22.   The price of success is hard work, dedication to the job at hand, and the determination that, whether we win or lose, we have applied the best of ourselves to the task at hand.

—Vice Lombardi

23.   I care not what others think of what I do, but I care very much about what I think of what I do! That is character!

—Theodore Roosevelt

24.   The ultimate measure of a man is not where he stands in moments of comfort, but where he stands at times of challenge and controversy.

—Martin Luther King, Jr.

25.   Ability may get you to the top, but it takes character to keep you there.

—John Wooden

26. What lies behind you and what lies in front of you pales in comparison to what lies inside of you.

—Ralph Waldo Emerson

27. Faced with crisis, the man of character falls back on himself. He imposes his own stamp of action, takes responsibility for it, makes it his own.

—Charles de Gaulle

28. Disciplining yourself to do what you know is right and important, although difficult, is the highroad to pride, self-esteem, and personal satisfaction.

—Margaret Thatcher

29. People grow through experience if they meet life honestly and courageously. This is how character is built.

—Eleanor Roosevelt

30. Our character is what we do when we think no one is looking.

—H. Jackson Brown, Jr.

A LESSON FROM A STORY

Things which matter most must never be at the mercy of things which matter least.

—Goethe

High school is a hectic time; there is so much going on. Teens learn how to balance school, clubs, sports, and jobs into their schedule, and they are challenged to maintain high standards in all of them. I am an example of such a balancing act.

I juggle schoolwork, my duties as treasurer of the science club, and my job on a local dairy farm. On top of that, I am challenged to balance my role as an active member and reporter of our FFA chapter with my commitment to the high-school wrestling team. If you are familiar with either of these activities, you know exactly how much dedication and time they demand.

FFA and wrestling are two of the most important things in my high-school career. The earliest memories I have are of wrestling at biddy tournaments and helping my dad around our farm. Wrestling and agriculture are two things I've known all of my life. When November of my freshman year rolled around, I was faced with a difficult predicament. November marks the start of wrestling season, and it is also the beginning of parliamentary procedure practices for FFA. I had been looking forward to being on the parliamentary procedure team since I first learned about it in ag class over two months before. So I was faced with a choice—I had to choose between parliamentary procedure and wrestling.

I gave much thought to what I was going to do, and I finally reached a decision. I decided that from November through March I would focus the majority of my energy on wrestling, but from the end of March until October I would focus my time and attention on FFA. During wrestling season I am completely focused on wrestling. FFA is still very important, but it gets less attention. However, when wrestling season concludes, my mind switches gears, and my focus goes right back to my FFA commitments.

Deciding to focus on one thing at a time, whether it is wrestling or FFA, has allowed me to perform well in both. Within the same school year I was sectional wrestling champion at 119 pounds, and that May I received a gold rating for my reporter's scrapbook. I know that I was able to achieve those two honors because I chose to set priorities and honor my commitments.

Martin Overholt,
West Holmes FFA

How do you honor your priorities and commitments?

PERSONAL REFLECTIONS

Write your favorite quote from this chapter in the space below:

_____
_____
_____
_____
_____
_____
_____

Why is this quote especially meaningful to you?

_____
_____
_____
_____
_____
_____
_____

Reflect upon a goal that you are currently striving to achieve. Prioritize a list of your top ten to twelve values. Write your list in the space provided:

_____   _____
_____   _____
_____   _____
_____   _____
_____   _____
_____   _____
_____   _____
_____   _____
_____   _____

Consider the next goal on your list. What realignment of your values list will be necessary?

_____
_____
_____
_____
_____
_____

Chapter 3

Following MapQuest Directions

Planning and Taking Action

Plan your work for today and every day, then work your plan.

—Norman Vincent Peale

How many times have you consulted the Internet for directions before starting your journey to a new destination? MapQuest[1] is just one of many Web sites that provides travel directions and maps to help you get from one place to another. Sites such as this give you routes based on the shortest distance or shortest travel time and can customize directions if you want to avoid highways and toll roads.

Advanced planning makes your trip less stressful and more enjoyable. Goals are like the directions on your MapQuest printout. As each goal is met, you can assess progress and see how far you have traveled. As such, goals are mile markers on your success journey.

A global positioning system (GPS) provides an additional form of travel guidance. Many people often rely on the computerized voice that tells them, "Prepare to turn left in point two miles." And when they miss their turn, it is so reassuring to hear, "Recalculating route." They know their GPS is making the necessary adjustments to get them back on track. But directions, and even the best GPS device, won't get you to your destination. Is the gas tank full? Are you well rested and ready to drive? Do you understand the directions, or do you have a navigator traveling with you? The bottom line is that both preparation and action are required.

PREPARATION BEGINS WITH PLANNING

Bobby Knight, the famed collegiate basketball coach known for his temper and fiery personality, once said, "The will to succeed is important, but what's more important is the will to prepare." Planning is an essential part of preparation. Having been a high-school family and consumer sciences teacher, I have had many opportunities to help students organize school programs, conduct community service projects, and prepare for skill-event competitions. Our work was always guided by the five-step planning process outlined below:

Identify concerns: Be aware of situations that are troublesome to you. Consider what changes are needed in your personal or family life, work or school environment, and community. Think about the kind of difference you want to make. Prioritize your list of concerns.

Set a goal: Remember to create *SMART* goals. Think of your goal as the picture on the box of a jigsaw puzzle and the tasks that need to be completed as the individual puzzle pieces. Always keep the picture in front of you.

Form a plan: How do you go about putting together a thousand-piece puzzle? I personally follow the same plan each time I start a new puzzle. I begin by setting a limit of thirty minutes to an hour as the length of time I will spend on the activity. First, I pick out all the pieces with a straight edge and assemble the border. I proceed by sorting the remaining pieces into predominate color groupings, and, with the picture as my guide, I assemble sections together. Just like putting together a puzzle, working on any goal requires a plan. List the resources and materials needed. Identify tasks that need to be completed, and prioritize the order in which they will be finished. Establish a timeline. Decide if you will enlist assistance from others or whether you can even delegate tasks. Consider how you will assess your progress along the way.

Act on the plan: Do what needs to be done. Throughout the New Testament of the Bible, Jesus frequently taught his followers by telling stories or parables. The idea of personal responsibility for taking action is addressed in Matthew 25:14–30, in what is commonly known as the parable of the talents. Jesus tells the story of three servants who were given responsibility to look after their master's money (coins called talents) while he was away on a journey. One of the servants was given five talents, one received two talents, and a third was entrusted with a single talent. During the master's absence, the first two servants invested their talents and doubled the amount they had been given. The last servant simply dug a hole and buried his talent, because he was fearful of his master's reputation for being a harsh and judgmental man. By burying the talent, he reasoned, he would at least be able to return what he had been given without causing a loss. Upon the master's return, the three servants were called to account for the talents they had been given. The successful servants were rewarded for their efforts and given additional responsibility.

When the last servant was called, he blamed the master for his fear and simply returned the single talent. The master chastised him for being wicked and lazy, and he told the servant that the money should have at least been deposited with the bankers to earn interest. The servant learned the valuable lesson that responsibility requires action.

Follow-up: Many people work through a "to do" list and move on to another goal without taking time for reflection and follow-up. Important learning takes place when you assess the results of planning and action. Ask yourself these key questions: How did I know that I achieved my goal? What challenges did I face? How did I overcome them? What have I learned from this experience that will benefit me and others in the future?

GETTING STARTED

Success depends on planning your work and then working your plan. In his book, *Your Road Map for Success,* leadership expert and author John Maxwell describes the success journey in the following way:

> When you commit yourself to your dream and express it in achievable goals, you provide yourself with a visual reminder of where you're going and how you hope to get there. It's part of the success process: Your dream determines your goals. Your goals map out your actions. Your actions create results. And the results bring you success.[2]

Life is full of uncertainties. There may be numerous occasions when you, like the third servant in the parable of the talents, are fearful of making a mistake, and so you do nothing. Unfortunately, some people are willing to let opportunities pass them by, if the path is not well defined and the outcome is not a guaranteed success. They are content to wait on the sidelines just hoping that success finds them.

Successful people, however, have learned not to wait. They are willing to take the first step, despite the unknown. Dr. Martin Luther King, Jr., said it best. "Take the first step in faith. You don't have to see the whole staircase. Just take the first step." Something happens when we commit ourselves to doing something. Once we are in motion, it becomes much easier to take the next step. We gain more confidence and competence in the process. The momentum grows as a result of that first step.

In his book, *The Success Principles: How to Get from Where You Are to Where You Want to Be,* author Jack Canfield offers a powerful example of taking action. He describes holding up a one-hundred-dollar bill during a seminar presentation and asking, "Who wants this hundred-dollar bill?" As you can imagine, lots of people raised their hands, and some even shouted out that they wanted the money. But he just stood there patiently holding out the money until they *got it.* Someone eventually jumped from her chair, rushed to the front of the room, and took the money from his hand. He continued by saying, "What did this person do that no one else in the room did? She got off her butt and took action. She did what was necessary to get the money. And that is exactly what you must do if you want to succeed in life. You must take action, and, in most cases, the sooner the better."[3] So, what are you waiting for? Get busy.

SUCCESSFUL PEOPLE DON'T FIND TIME—THEY MAKE TIME

Another critical factor that contributes to success is how we choose to use our time. The people who succeed in life value time as one of their greatest resources. They understand that time is not really something to be managed. You can't take three hours from today and add it to tomorrow. Everyone gets the same twenty-four hours in each day. What *can* be managed, however, is your *use* of time. What you *do* with time defines your life. Alan Lakein, a noted time management expert, hit the mark when he said, "Time is life. It is irreversible and irreplaceable. To waste your time is to waste your life, but to master your time is to master your life and make the most of it."

One of my biggest pet peeves is when people claim they don't have time to do something. What they really mean is that they either are not a good manager of time or they really don't want to do something in the first place. There really is no such thing as lack of time. You have plenty of time to do everything you really *want* to do. The key is not in *finding* time but rather in *making* time to accomplish the important things that have high value and priority. Successful people use a variety of strategies for managing their use of time. Consider implementing the following five strategies.

1. *Plan Your Day:* Contractors have building plans, executives have business plans, coaches have game plans, and successful people have daily plans. Begin by setting aside ten minutes each day (the night before or first thing in the morning) to write down the things you want to accomplish. Number or list them in order of importance, and keep your list visible throughout the day. You will be amazed at how much more productive you become. Check off each item when you've completed it, and assess your progress throughout the day. A sense of accomplishment is one of the best feelings you can have.

2. *Make an Appointment:* A simple solution for procrastination is to make an appointment with yourself. Make the decision that something is going to get done, decide when you are going to do it, and commit yourself to that specific time. For example, you have a report for class or work that requires three hours of work, and your deadline is next Thursday. Ordinarily you might say, "I have until next week to get that report done," but there is a huge difference when you say instead, "I will complete the report on Tuesday between 3:00 and 6:00 PM." You reinforce the commitment when you go one step further and record it in an electronic planner or write it on your daily calendar. Make it a habit to work ahead of the deadline. Plan to work for thirty minutes on something that isn't due that day. In

addition to overcoming procrastination, this simple strategy helps you develop self-discipline and reduce stress.

3. *Schedule Time for Routine Tasks:* One of easiest ways to manage routine tasks is to block out a specific time in your daily schedule. This works best when you can set aside the same time period each day. The key is being consistent and forming a habit. Responding to e-mail and text messages is a perfect example. I know people who are obsessed with electronic communication. If their phone buzzes with a text message, or a new e-mail message alert pops up on their computer screen, they stop whatever they are doing to read and respond. What a distraction! Consider reducing interruptions by making it a general practice to read and respond to e-mail or text messages only at designated times, such as first thing in the morning, at lunch break, and near the end of the day.

4. *Know Your Most Productive Time:* All people have an internal body clock or rhythm. There seems to be a certain time during the day when a person is the most productive. I am sure you have heard someone say, "I am definitely a morning person," while someone else says, "Not me, I'm a night owl." It is important to recognize your own clock and know when you function most efficiently and creatively. Use that knowledge when developing your daily plan. Schedule yourself, whenever possible, to do the most important work during your peak hours.

5. *Learn to Say No:* Once you have a plan, protect it. Highly successful people say no frequently—to extra assignments, to other people's emergencies, and to requests that don't align with their priorities. Many times you can get wrapped up in projects and opportunities that are merely good, and you have no time left for the really great experiences that provide huge personal or professional benefits. Remember, sometimes you have to say no to the good so that you can say yes to the great.

When you understand that time is your life, it becomes imperative to figure out ways to make the most of it. Success depends on effective use of time. Begin with careful planning, and follow through with committed action.

SUMMING IT UP

- The success journey requires both planning and action.

- Consider adopting a process for planning that includes identifying concerns, setting goals, forming plans, acting, and following up.

- Successful people do not let the fear of making a mistake keep them from taking action. They are willing to take the first step, despite the unknown.

- Taking action helps you gain confidence, competence, and momentum.

- Successful people value time as one of their greatest resources. They make time to accomplish what is important.

- Five basic strategies for managing your use of time include:

    - Plan Your Day

    - Make an Appointment

    - Schedule Time for Routine Tasks

    - Know Your Most Productive Time

    - Learn to Say No

- Success depends on effective use of time. Begin with careful planning, and follow through with committed action.

Be wise, and remember the Chinese proverb that says, "A journey of ten thousand miles begins with that very first step." Dust off your MapQuest instructions and get moving.

WORDS OF WISDOM

1. Setting a goal is not the main thing. It is deciding how you will go about achieving it and staying with that plan.

    —Tom Landry

2. Before anything else, getting ready is the secret of success.

    —Henry Ford

3. You see, in life, lots of people know what to do, but few people actually do what they know. Knowing is not enough! You must take action.

    —Tony Robbins

4. The elevator to success is out of order. You'll have to use the stairs ... one step at a time.

    —Joe Girard

5. Developing the plan is actually laying out the sequence of events that have to occur for you to achieve your goal.

    —George Morrisey

6.   There are risks and costs to action. But they are far less than the long-range risks of comfortable inaction.

—John F. Kennedy

7.   The secret to getting ahead is getting started. The secret of getting started is breaking your complex, overwhelming tasks into small, manageable tasks, and then starting on the first one.

—Mark Twain

8.   Let our advance worrying become advance thinking and planning.

—Winston Churchill

9.   It isn't sufficient just to want—you've got to ask yourself what you are going to do to get the things you want.

—Franklin D. Roosevelt

10.   Decide what you want, decide what you are willing to exchange for it. Establish your priorities and go to work.

—H. L. Hunt

11.   By failing to prepare, you are preparing to fail.

—Benjamin Franklin

12.   Inaction breeds doubt and fear. Action breeds confidence and courage. If you want to conquer fear, do not sit home and think about it. Go out and get busy.

—Dale Carnegie

13.   A goal without an action plan is a daydream.

—Nathaniel Branden

14.   I've always believed that if you put in the work, the results will come. I don't do things halfheartedly. Because I know if I do, then I can expect halfhearted results.

—Michael Jordan

15.   I will prepare, and some day my chance will come.

—Abraham Lincoln

16.   Action is a great restorer and builder of confidence. ... Perhaps the action you take will be successful; perhaps different action or adjustments will have to follow. But any action is better than no action at all.

—Norman Vincent Peale

17.   Never leave that till tomorrow which you can do today.

—Benjamin Franklin

18.   Planning is bringing the future into the present, so that you can do something about it now.

—Alan Lakein

19.   The time to repair the roof is when the sun is shining.

—John F. Kennedy

20.   The world needs dreamers, and the world needs doers. But above all, the world needs dreamers who do.

—Sarah Ban Breathnach

21.   When it is obvious that the goals cannot be reached, don't adjust the goals; adjust the action steps.

—Confucius

22.   The way to get started is to quit talking and begin doing.

—Walt Disney

23.   Our goals can only be reached through a vehicle of a plan, in which we must fervently believe, and upon which we must vigorously act. There is no other route to success.

—Pablo Picasso

24.   People who reach their potential and fulfill their dreams determine and act on their priorities daily.

—John Maxwell

25.   Nothing is particularly hard if you divide it into small jobs.

—Henry Ford

26.   It's incredibly easy to get caught up in an activity trip, in the busyness of life, to work harder and harder at climbing the ladder of success only to discover it's leaning against the wrong wall.

—Stephen Covey

27.   For every minute you take to plan ahead, you save five minutes down the road. That's a 500-percent return for the time invested.

—Debbie Macomber

28.   Action is the foundational key to success.

—Pablo Picasso

29.   It is hard to fail, but it is worse never to have tried to succeed. In this life, we get nothing save by effort.

—Theodore Roosevelt

30.   The bad news is time flies. The good news is you're the pilot.

—Michael Althsuler

A LESSON FROM A STORY

You must take action now that will move you toward your goals. Develop a sense of urgency in your life.

—H. Jackson Brown, Jr.

I'm a third-generation Buckeye fan. I attended my first Ohio State football game with my grandfather when I was seven years old, but it was during the fall of fifth grade that I really noticed the marching band. I will always remember how the band brought people out of their seats. The roar of the crowd, especially during "Script Ohio," made a huge impression on me, and I knew I wanted to be a member of that band.

As a freshman in the state FFA band, I was seated with the other band members before the convention's general session. Stewart Kitchen, the drum major of the OSU marching band, was awaiting his introduction as guest speaker. I didn't know if I would ever have an opportunity to personally meet Stew again, so I jumped at the chance to go backstage and introduce myself. I shared with him that I wanted to be a member of the marching band when I attended college at Ohio State, and he encouraged me to work hard and pursue my goal.

I've had several opportunities to talk with Stew since meeting him at the state FFA convention. He has helped me to understand that achieving my goal will greatly depend on what I do now to develop my skills as a musician as well as the amount of work I put in to learning the marching drills.

With that in mind, I participate in marching, jazz, concert, and pep band activities at school. I also participate in a community band, and I have attended a summer band clinic at Ohio State. There are no guarantees that I will be successful, but I truly believe that the actions I take now will help me to one day be a member of the OSU marching band.

Clay Garrett,
Eastern Brown FFA

What action must you take now to achieve your long-term goal?

PERSONAL REFLECTIONS

Write your favorite quote from this chapter in the space below:

_____
_____
_____
_____
_____
_____
_____
_____
_____

Why is this quote especially meaningful to you?

_____
_____
_____
_____
_____
_____
_____
_____
_____

Consider a goal that you have recently set for yourself. Brainstorm a list of action steps that you must complete in order to successfully achieve the goal:

1. _____
2. _____
3. _____
4. _____

What strategy will you use to help you manage your time?

_____
_____
_____
_____
_____
_____

Chapter 4

Selecting Music for the Drive

Monitoring Your Self-Talk and Attitude

You are what you are because of what goes into your mind.

—Zig Ziglar

One of our most memorable family vacations has been a three-week road trip to explore the western part of the United States. The trip from Ohio took us through fourteen states and as far west as Las Vegas. In order to see as much as we did in such a short period of time, we were constantly on the go. Needless to say, the grass did not have time to grow beneath our feet.

Our passenger van was our home away from home, as we racked up the miles, and music kept us entertained along the way. One of our family rules is that the driver gets to select the music. Finding a radio station can be a real challenge when you are on the road in unfamiliar territory, so we went prepared with a collection of our favorite CDs.

Have you ever really thought about how music affects you? I speak from experience when I say that it is not wise to drive on the open plains and listen to rock music unless you have the cruise control set, and that classical music and Broadway show tunes are not recommended for night driving when you are tired. Music has a very powerful way of affecting you physically, mentally, and emotionally. But music isn't the only thing you may listen to daily.

You are constantly bombarded with messages from the media, entertainment sources, friends, family, and co-workers. I don't know about you, but I am guilty of even talking to myself. Just as the driver had the choice to select the music we listened to while on vacation, successful individuals realize and understand that they have the ability to choose the messages that will influence and affect them.

BEING AWARE OF OUR OWN THOUGHTS

From the classic titled *As a Man Thinketh*, written in 1904 by James Allen, readers gain a timeless lesson regarding the importance of controlling our thoughts. At the heart of his message Allen says:

> Just as the gardener cultivates his plot, keeping it free from weeds, and growing the flowers and fruits which he requires, so may a man tend the garden of his mind, weeding out all the wrong, useless, and impure thoughts, and cultivating toward perfection the flowers and fruits of right, useful, and pure thought.[1]

If you know someone who has a vegetable garden or loves to landscape, you know they take great pride and pleasure in watching plants bloom and grow. But just planting them is not enough; the garden requires care and upkeep. The plants need water and fertilizer, and you may need to pull weeds.

In Allen's analogy your mind is the garden. You must be on the lookout for those pesky weeds that pop into your mind in the form of fear, doubt, and negative thoughts. If you don't remove them quickly and regularly, they will take over and destroy your self-confidence and choke your potential for achieving success. If you remove the weeds in your mind regularly, the flowers and fruits which represent your positive and productive thoughts will have room to grow.

THE POWER OF VISUALIZATION

It is fascinating to consider how the mind works. Take just a moment to close your eyes and think about home. Go ahead and do it now. Did the letters h-o-m-e flash before your mind's eye or did you envision the outside of your house? Maybe you saw yourself in a particular room, such as the kitchen, living room, or bedroom. This simple exercise demonstrates that your thoughts are based on images rather than words. Armed with that knowledge, you can learn to use your mind as a tool to help you accomplish your goals.

Sports psychologists have helped professional athletes improve their performance by using a technique called visualization. Visualization is the process whereby you "see" yourself doing something successfully before you actually try it. Tiger Woods can picture in his mind making a birdie shot before the putter hits the golf ball. Venus Williams can see herself serving an ace in a tennis match, and Ken Griffey, Jr., can visualize the bat making contact before the pitcher even releases the baseball. These athletes are filling their minds with positive and productive thoughts. Michael Jordan once said, "I never looked at the consequences of missing a big shot … when you think about the consequences you always think of a negative result." What do you think he visualized? My guess is nothing but net!

Successful individuals have a vision, a clear picture in their minds, about something important that they will accomplish in the future. People who develop this skill not only envision themselves achieving, they habitually rehearse it in their minds. The more clearly and more often they picture themselves doing it, the closer they move toward fulfilling their dreams.

Likewise, you are pulled in the direction of your thoughts, whether they are positive or negative. In general, people who succeed regularly expect to succeed. They begin by developing the habit of expecting good things to happen. The type of person you become begins with your thoughts, and your attitude shows others what you are thinking. It all starts in the mind. Our images are great motivators.

CHOOSING OUR ATTITUDE

While surfing the Internet for quotes I came across the following from Lowell Peacock at http://www.goodreads.com/quotes/show/102558. The quote reads, "Attitude is the first quality that marks the successful man. If he has a positive attitude and is a positive thinker, who likes challenges and difficult situations, then he has half his success achieved." It isn't what happens that is most important; it is how you handle what happens that really counts.

How you handle anything in life begins with attitude—and attitude is a choice, regardless of the circumstances. Your attitude defines your outlook. Do you see the positive or negative in circumstances? Do you see you glass half full or half empty? Your attitude serves as a filter for your thinking process, and it influences how you respond in any given situation. In fact, your attitude, not your intelligence, talent, education, technical ability, opportunity, or even hard work, is the main factor that determines whether you can achieve your goals.[2]

For instance, consider how you might respond to feedback you are given for a report you present at school or on the job. Do you only expect to hear good comments, or are you open to suggestions for improvement? Successful individuals realize that there is as much useful data in negative feedback as there is in positive feedback.

It is helpful to know if you are off-course, headed in the wrong direction, or simply doing the wrong thing. Remember, feedback is simply information, and it comes from the personal perspective of another individual. Don't take it personally, and resist the temptation to argue, defend, or explain yourself. The most productive response is to say, "Thanks for taking the time to tell me what you see and how you feel. I appreciate it." That doesn't mean you agree with everything that has been said. It simply means you appreciate someone's honesty.

The key to dealing with negative feedback is to realize that you are ultimately in charge of deciding whether or not the information provided is helpful and has merit. Just because you may think something, or even hear it from someone else, does not necessarily mean it is true.

THE CASE FOR POSITIVE THINKING

Positive thinking has a nice ring to it, but, unfortunately, for most people it's really just wishful thinking. That is why positive thinking does not always work. In order to be productive, you must accompany positive thinking with a genuine belief.

People who succeed in life don't just think they can—they believe they can. Positive thinkers are aware of negative ideas clamoring for attention, but they won't allow themselves to be dragged down by them. Instead, they train themselves to choose a thought process that will move them toward their goals.

Computer programmers use an acronym called *GIGO,* which stands for garbage in, garbage out. The mind operates in a similar manner. Your brain needs to be fed and exercised with useful information in order to function at its peak level of performance. Positive thinkers know this. They are careful about selecting the information that is fed into their minds. They are also diligent about routinely taking out the garbage. Your ability to choose, especially to choose your own attitude, is a valuable resource to have with you on the success journey.

Does having a positive attitude give you a guarantee that you won't be faced with problems or challenges? Of course not! While you can't adjust every situation to fit your life perfectly, you *can* adjust your attitude to fit all situations. People with positive attitudes understand that even problems present them with opportunities for finding solutions.

Having a negative attitude and blaming others for your circumstances only stands in the way of coming up with the solutions that are needed for moving forward to accomplish your goals. If you are always looking for excuses for why things can't be done, you will never find the reasons why they can.

Successful individuals understand that opportunities are not based on luck or having the perfect circumstances. Opportunities abound when you have the right attitude, and choosing a positive attitude helps you identify options. Author John Maxwell sums it up best when he writes, "The quality of your life and the duration of your success journey depend on your attitude, and you are the only person in the world with the power to make it better."[3]

THE MESSAGES WE SEND TO OTHERS AND OURSELVES

Take a moment to consider the power behind the words you speak to others. Does your message come across like fingernails running down a blackboard, or does it sound like music to the listener? As young children, my siblings and I frequently heard our father say, "If you can't say anything nice, then don't say anything at all." As much as I hated to hear him use that phrase, I repeat it to my own sons frequently. It may take some longer than others, but ultimately most people learn that kind words cost little but accomplish much.

Richard M. DeVos, cofounder of Amway, once said, "Few things in the world are more powerful than a positive push. A smile. A word of optimism and hope. A 'you can do it' when things are tough." Just as we choose our attitude, we can also choose to give our words the power of affirmation.

To affirm means to look for and find the good in people. It means building others up and encouraging them with words that are both nurturing and supportive. More than fifty years ago, Dale Carnegie said, "Any fool can criticize, condemn, and complain—and most fools do." He understood a basic truth of human nature: when we do something well and are acknowledged for it, we are encouraged to do even better the next time. Sincere praise brings out the best in people.

There is no greater form of personal motivation than directing those affirming thoughts toward yourself. Paul J. Meyer, founder of Success Motivation International, and the man behind *Success* magazine, made a very intuitive statement when he said, "No matter who you are or what your age may be, if you want to achieve permanent, sustaining success, the motivation that will drive you toward that goal must come from within." Successful individuals don't wait for others to motivate them; they do it themselves. Begin now by choosing positive thinking as the internal music that accompanies you on your journey.

SUMMING IT UP

- If you do not quickly and regularly remove thoughts of fear, doubt, and negativity, they will take over and destroy your self-confidence and choke your potential for achieving success.

- Visualization is a thought process whereby you "see" yourself doing something successfully before you actually try it.

- How you handle anything in life begins with attitude; and attitude is a choice, regardless of the circumstances.

- Research has shown that your attitude, not your intelligence, talent, education, technical ability, opportunity, or even hard work, is the main factor that determines whether you can achieve your goals.

- The key to dealing with negative feedback is to realize that *you* are ultimately in charge of deciding whether or not the information provided is helpful and has merit.

- Your ability to choose, especially to choose your own attitude, is the one of the most important resources you have for making a successful life journey.

- There is no greater form of personal motivation than directing affirmative thoughts toward yourself.

Robert Collier, one of America's original success authors, once said, "Your chances of success in any undertaking can always be measured by your belief in yourself." What you tell yourself, and how you process information from others, makes a difference. Make positive thinking the cornerstone of a strong belief in yourself.

WORDS OF WISDOM

1.   Your attitude, not your aptitude, will determine your altitude.

—Zig Ziglar

2.   The greatest discovery of all time is that a person can change his future by merely changing his attitude.

—Oprah Winfrey

3.   Change always starts first in your mind. The way you think determines the way you feel, and the way you feel influences the way you act.

—Rick Warren

4.   There are no constraints on the human mind, no walls around the human spirit, no barriers to our progress—except those we ourselves erect.

—Ronald Reagan

5.   No one can make you feel inferior without your consent.

—Eleanor Roosevelt

6.   If constructive thoughts are planted, positive outcomes will be the result. Plant the seeds of failure, and failure will follow.

—Sidney Madwed

7.   The secret of living a life of excellence is merely a matter of thinking thoughts of excellence. Really, it's a matter of programming our minds with the kind of information that will set us free.

—Charles R. Swindoll

8.   If you believe you can, you probably can. If you believe you won't, you most assuredly won't. Belief is the ignition switch that gets you off the launching pad.

—Denis Waitley

9.   You have to expect things of yourself before you can do them.

—Michael Jordan

10.   Life's battles don't always go to the stronger or faster man. But sooner or later the man who wins is the man who thinks he can.

—Vince Lombardi

11. Anybody can do just about anything with himself that he really wants to and makes up his mind to do. We are capable of greater things than we realize.

—Norman Vincent Peale

12. The greatest discovery of any generation is that a human being can alter his life by altering his attitude.

—William James

13. Whatever you vividly imagine, ardently desire, sincerely believe, and enthusiastically act upon ... must inevitably come to pass!

—Paul J. Meyer

14. Whatever we expect with confidence becomes our own self-fulfilling prophecy.

—Brian Tracy

15. Nurture your mind with great thoughts, for you will never go any higher than you think.

—Benjamin Disraeli

16.   The winners in life think constantly in terms of "I can," "I will," and "I am." Losers, on the other hand, concentrate their waking thoughts on what they should have or would have done, or what they can't do.

—Denis Waitley

17.   Whether you think you can or think you can't—you are right.

—Henry Ford

18.   You are today where your thoughts have brought you; you will be tomorrow where your thoughts take you.

—James Allen

19.   Enthusiasm and ambition are contagious. Positive people condition us for success the same way that positive thinking moves us forward to reach our goals.

—Debbie Macomber

20.   We become what we think about. Our minds are the steering mechanisms of our lives.

—Earl Nightingale

21.   People who succeed regularly expect to succeed. They develop the habit of expecting good things to happen, and they know that the primary vehicle for taking them where they want to go is the mind.

—Hal Urban

22.   You cannot tailor-make the situations in life, but you can tailor-make the attitudes to fit those situations.

—Zig Ziglar

23.   All that a man achieves or fails to achieve is the direct result of his thoughts.

—James Allen

24.   To accomplish great things, we must not only act, but also dream; not only plan, but also believe.

—Anatole France

25.   You are a living magnet. What you attract into your life is in harmony with your dominant thoughts.

—Brian Tracy

26.   Your living is determined not so much by what life brings to you as by the attitude you bring to life; not so much by what happens to you as by the way your mind looks at what happens.

—John Homer Miller

27.   People become really remarkable when they start thinking they can do things. When they believe in themselves, they have the first secret of success.

—Norman Vincent Peale

28.   What you think of yourself is much more important than what others think of you.

—Lucius Seneca

29.   You can be anything you want to be, if only you believe with sufficient conviction and act in accordance with your faith; for whatever the mind can conceive and believe the mind can achieve.

—Napoleon Hill

30.   Perpetual optimism is a force multiplier.

—Colin Powell

A LESSON FROM A STORY

Winners make a habit of manufacturing their own positive expectations in advance of the event.

—Brian Tracy

FFA's Camp Muskingum should be considered a top destination for all of Ohio's FFA members. If you are from another state, I am sure your state also sponsors a similar leadership camp.

Before my first trip to Camp Muskingum, I was very nervous, thinking about what other FFA members would be like. When our bus pulled up to camp that hot summer day, a mixed feeling of fear and excitement came over me. I watched the reactions of other members as they arrived. Some looked nervous and bug-eyed, just like me. I always thought I was social and easygoing, but were they? I was taking a huge risk, but I was determined at the beginning to have a great camp experience.

As the week went by my question was answered, and I realized I was in good company. Yes, there were many different people from around the state, but they all wanted to have fun and meet new people. I realized we had the same positive FFA attitude running through our veins. I have never seen so many people treat each other with kindness and respect.

I especially remember the last night at camp, when we had a campfire. A girl stood up and spoke with great emotion in her voice. She said she had been terrified to come to camp. About a month prior to Muskingum she had been kicked in the face by a horse. The incident had left a large scar on the side of her face. Holding back tears, she said that if she had known how kind FFA members from all over Ohio were, she would not have been so scared. The response she received from others had made her feel as if the scar was never there.

That week at camp I realized how very proud I was to wear the blue corduroy jacket that symbolizes opportunity for the nation's greatest youth organization. Being an FFA member has transformed me into a better communicator and person. This organization has taught me to set my goals high and to look for the best in every situation. But most of all, FFA has taught me how people should treat their peers.

Branton Duncan,
West Holmes FFA

What attitude do you choose to adopt before you meet new people or embark on new experiences?

PERSONAL REFLECTIONS

Write your favorite quote from this chapter in the space below:

_____

_____

_____

_____

_____

_____

_____

Why is this quote especially meaningful to you?

_____

_____

_____

_____

_____

_____

_____

_____

_____

Create a vision board or goal book. List all the things you want to achieve, and illustrate your goals with pictures. A peg-board, poster board, or three-ring binder are great organizers. Practice the technique of visualization.

Reflect on a problem situation that you have recently experienced. Did you respond with a positive or negative attitude? How might you have changed your response?

_____

_____

_____

_____

_____

_____

_____

_____

_____

Chapter 5

Choosing a Fork in the Road

Knowing What It Means to Lead

You have brains in your head, and feet in your shoes. You can steer yourself any direction you choose.

—Dr. Seuss

Have you ever traveled in a caravan of vehicles headed to the same destination? In January 2008 my sister and I made a road trip to New Orleans to watch the Ohio State Buckeyes play against the Louisiana State Tigers in college football's BCS National Championship game. We left Cincinnati at 5:00 on a Friday evening and headed south. Our plans were to drive straight through the night and arrive at the home of our aunt and uncle in Slidell, Louisiana, around 8:00 on Saturday morning.

At some point south of Louisville, on Interstate 65, we caught up with a Lincoln Navigator with Ohio license plates. It was quite obvious that they were headed toward our destination, since the message on their rear window proudly declared, "New Orleans Bound—Go Bucks!!" As we approached Nashville, we were passed by another car from Ohio decked out with OSU window flags. After readjusting the cruise control, our three vehicles stayed together in a pack for several hours as we traveled south.

When we got to Birmingham, Alabama, things changed. As we made our way around the city, we had the option of staying on I-65 or exiting on I-59 to head southwest. At the fork in the road, the driver of the lead car stayed in I-65, while we followed the Navigator onto the ramp for I-59. I can only speculate why the lead car didn't take our route. The driver could have been following a different set of directions. Maybe they were picking up friends or family on the way. They might even have had reservations at a downtown hotel for the night. We continued to follow the Navigator until it exited at Meridian, Mississippi, and we were on our own for the remainder of the trip to Slidell.

Achieving your goals in life is a lot like that road trip to Louisiana. You will discover that more than one path leads to success. Sometimes you will pursue goals with the support of others, while other times you may have to go it alone. Regardless of whether you find yourself in the front, middle, rear, or even without a title, you will have opportunities to lead.

DEFINING LEADERSHIP

Former president Dwight D. Eisenhower once said, "Leadership is the art of getting someone else to do something you want done because he wants to do it." When you first read that quote it may strike you that leadership sounds a lot like manipulation. While it is true that the misuse of leadership for selfish gains can indeed be manipulation, respected and effective leaders understand that leadership is more about *influence* rather than manipulation.

So, who do you consider to be the leaders that influence? Any number of people could be included on that list. Presidents and other governmental officials, chief executive officers of Fortune 500 companies, PTO or other community service organization officers, and even your supervisor at work may readily come to mind. Perhaps it is a simple oversight, but I would guess that most people don't include their own name on that list.

But who else do you know has greater influence over the personal decisions you make on a daily basis? Begin today to consider yourself the CEO of your own life. You have within you the power to make significant choices. If you don't like where you are heading, then set out in a new direction today. No one is forcing you to do any of the following: choose a particular post-secondary program of study, show up for work at a job that is not rewarding, spend your free time in a certain way, or maintain unhealthy personal relationships. These are all examples of choices you make.

Author Mark Sanborn delivers a very insightful message simply in the title of his book *You Don't Need a Title to Be a Leader.* According to Sanborn, "The bottom line is influence and inspiration come from the person, not the position." He further states, "When you do your job—any job—with initiative and determination to make a positive difference, you become a leader."[1]

Throughout the years, it has often been debated whether leaders are born or made. Are the qualities of effective leadership linked to genes that are inherited, or are they actually skills that can be learned and developed? Many agree with Vince Lombardi, legendary football coach of the Green Bay Packers when he says, *"Leaders are made; they are not born. They are made by hard effort, which is the price all of us must pay to achieve any goal that is worthwhile."*

QUALITIES OF LEADERSHIP

You can't effectively lead others until you can first lead yourself. According to Mark Sanborn, personal leadership requires the qualities of character, competence, and connection. Character traits such as honesty, integrity, and respect describe who you are as a person. Competency traits describe your knowledge base and technical skills, while connection skills relate to your ability to communicate and build relationships with others.

Over the years, I have attended numerous workshops and seminars that have addressed the topic of leadership development. On several occasions I have been asked to identify the personal qualities and skills needed for effective leadership by creating an acronym for the word leadership. My acrostic has often changed depending upon the leader I use as my source of inspiration, but I have found the list to be more meaningful when I think about a leader I admire and know personally. Along with the following sample acronym, I have included a quote to help express the value of each quality:

L   Loyalty:

You must, of course, have the courage to be loyal to those you lead. Doing so is not always easy. It starts, however, with loyalty to yourself —your standards, your system, your values.

—John Wooden

E   Enthusiasm:

As a leader, you must be filled with energy and eagerness, joy and love for what you do. If you lack enthusiasm for your job, you cannot perform to the best of your ability.

—John Wooden

A   Action oriented:

A leader must have initiative—the courage to make a decision, to act, and the willingness and strength to risk failure and take a stand, even when it goes against the opinion of others.

—John Wooden

D   Disciplined:

Do something every day that you don't want to do; this is the golden rule for acquiring the habit of doing your duty without pain.

—Mark Twain

E Example:

Your own personal example is one of the most powerful leadership tools you possess. Put it to good use: be what you want your team to become.

—John Wooden

R Resourcefulness:

Cooperation—the sharing of ideas, information, creativity, responsibilities, and tasks—is a priority of good leadership.

—John Wooden

S Servanthood:

Life's most urgent question is: What are you doing for others?

—Martin Luther King, Jr.

H Honesty:

We need to be honest, not because of what might happen to us when we're not, but because of what happens inside of us when we are.

—Hal Urban

I Integrity:

As a leader, you must be sincerely committed to what's right rather than who's right.

—John Wooden

P Purpose-mindedness:

Without a clear purpose, you have no foundation on which you base decisions, allocate your time, and use your resources.

—Rick Warren

In no way does this acronym include all the qualities of an effective leader. Another person completing this exercise might identify other qualities, such as **l**istener, **e**ngaging, **a**mbitious, **d**irectional, **e**nergetic, **r**esponsible, **s**incere, **h**ardworking, **i**ndependent, and **p**roblem-solver. Creating an acronym provides an opportunity for personal reflection, and reviewing your own list may help you to identify areas for skill development and improvement. Remember, leadership skills *can* be developed through study and practice. Be sure to check out the recommended reading list at the end of this book for additional insights.

LEADING FROM THE FRONT

Many people think of a leader as the "titled" person for a group or organization. Teachers are leaders in classrooms. Chief executive officers are leaders of companies. A president can lead a civic organization or an entire nation. Even the car with the window flags held the position of caravan leader during our road trip to Louisiana.

When leading from the front, you must establish a vision for the group and unite the followers in supporting and upholding that vision. This highly visible leader must determine priorities, allocate resources, plan for staff or member development, and delegate assignments to others. The leader in the front carries the responsibility for success or failure of the entire organization.

LEADING FROM THE MIDDLE

Some of the most powerful people in organizations do not hold titles, and they are not even responsible for making the crucial decisions. Instead, these individuals lead from the middle by sharing their knowledge and expertise with decision makers. These individuals are creative thinkers and problem solvers.

At one point during our trip to New Orleans, the driver of the Navigator saw a problem with the direction the lead driver was taking and made a necessary route adjustment. In a similar fashion, leaders in the middle may be called upon for input or may even be asked to recommend a change. In addition to needing critical thinking skills, a person leading from the middle requires both confidence and sensitivity when sharing ideas.

LEADING FROM THE REAR

All successful leaders have learned that before they can lead others, they must be able to lead themselves. You never know when you will have the opportunity to be out in front. When I think back to the caravan experience of our road trip, I remember that most of the time we were in the rear. But when the driver of the Navigator exited at Meridian, Mississippi, we were prepared to take the lead. We had our own map and set of directions, and after stopping to refill both the fuel tank and my sister's coffee mug, we had no problem reaching Slidell, Louisiana.

In his book *The 360° Leader* John Maxwell writes, "Leadership is a choice you make, not a place you sit. Anyone can choose to become a leader wherever he is. You can make a difference no matter where you are."[2]

Begin searching for ways to make life better for yourself and those around you. As John Wooden once said, "When opportunity comes, it's too late to prepare." Work hard now to develop personal relationships, identify and live according to your values, improve communication skills, increase self-discipline, establish goals, create action plans for achieving those goals, and hold yourself accountable for results.

SUMMING IT UP

Key points from this chapter include:

- The ability to provide leadership is available regardless of whether you are in the front, middle, or rear.

- Respected and effective leaders understand that leadership is about having the ability to *influence*, rather than manipulate, others.

- Leadership skills can be learned and developed through study and practice.

- Creating an acrostic for the word *leadership* provides an opportunity for personal reflection. Reviewing your own list may help to identify areas for skill development and improvement.

- When leading from the front, you must establish a vision for the group and unite the followers in supporting and upholding that vision.

- Leading from the middle involves sharing your knowledge and expertise with decision makers.

- All successful leaders have learned that before they can lead others, they must be able to lead themselves.

Mark Sanborn writes, "When you act as a leader, you exercise control over your life and help to influence and inspire those around you."[3] Now, which fork in the road are you prepared to choose? It is up to you to lead the way.

WORDS OF WISDOM

1. The most essential quality for leadership is not perfection, but credibility. People must be able to trust you, or they won't follow you.

    —Rick Warren

2. A good objective of leadership is to help those who are doing poorly to do well and to help those who are doing well to do even better.

    —Jim Rohn

3. In simplest terms, a leader is one who knows where he wants to go, and gets up, and goes.

    —John Erksine

4. Leadership is seeing the possibilities in a situation while others are seeing the limitations.

    —John Maxwell

5. Ultimately, I believe that's what leadership is all about: helping others to achieve their own greatness by helping the organization to succeed.

    —John Wooden

6.   The supreme quality for leadership is unquestionably integrity. Without it, no real success is possible, no matter whether it is on a section gang, a football field, in an army, or in an office.

—Dwight D. Eisenhower

7.   One person can make a difference, and every person should try.

—John F. Kennedy

8.   The first responsibility of a leader is to define reality. The last is to say thank you. In between, the leader is a servant.

—Max De Pree

9.   The very essence of leadership is that you have a vision. It's got to be a vision you can articulate clearly and forcefully on every occasion. You can't blow an uncertain trumpet.

—Theodore Hesburgh

10.   The difference between a boss and a leader: a boss says, "Go!"—a leader says, "Let's go"!

—E. M. Kelly

11.   There are many qualities that make a great leader. But having strong beliefs, being able to stick with them through popular and unpopular times, is the most important characteristic of a great leader.

—Rudy Giuliani

12.   Great leaders are almost always great simplifiers who can cut through argument, debate and doubt, to offer a solution everybody can understand.

—Colin Powell

13.   No man will make a great leader who wants to do it all himself or get all the credit for doing it.

—Andrew Carnegie

14.   Always do everything you ask of those you command.

—George S. Patton

15.   Your job as a leader is to see that everyone has a role in your group or organization and that he or she recognizes the importance of that role.

—Napoleon Hill

16.   Nothing so conclusively proves a man's ability to lead others as what he does from day to day to lead himself.

—Thomas Watson

17.   The growth and development of people is the highest calling of a leader.

—Dale Galloway

18.   Good leaders make people feel that they're at the very heart of things, not at the periphery. Everyone feels that he or she makes a difference to the success of the organization. When that happens, people feel centered, and that gives their work meaning.

—Warren G. Bennis

19.   The best leaders are very often the best listeners. They have an open mind. They are not interested in having their own way but in finding the best way.

—Wilfred Peterson

20.   Do not go where the path may lead; go instead where there is no path, and leave a trail.

—Ralph Waldo Emerson

21.   The world will belong to passionate, driven leaders... people
      who not only have enormous amounts of energy, but who can
      energize those whom they lead.

                                                    —Jack Welch

22.   Leadership is inspiring others with a vision of what they can
      contribute.

                                                  —John Maxwell

23.   The ultimate leader is one who is willing to develop people to
      the point that they eventually surpass him or her in knowledge
      and ability.

                                            —Fred A. Manske, Jr.

24.   The final test of a leader is that he leaves behind him in other
      men the conviction and the will to carry on.

                                              —Walter Lippmann

25.   If your actions inspire others to dream more, learn more, do
      more, and become more, you are a leader.

                                          —John Quincy Adams

26.   Good leaders are like baseball umpires: they go practically unnoticed when doing their jobs right.

—Byrd Baggett

27.   Leadership is the lifting of a man's vision to higher sights, the raising of a man's performance to a higher standard, the building of a man's personality beyond its normal limitations.

—Peter Drucker

28.   It is better to lead from behind and to put others in front, especially when you celebrate victory when nice things occur. You take the front line when there is danger. Then people will appreciate your leadership.

—Nelson Mandela

29.   Leadership is taking responsibility while others are making excuses.

—John Maxwell

30.   Your own personal example is one of the most powerful leadership tools you possess. Put it to good use: Be what you want your team to become.

—John Wooden

A LESSON FROM A STORY

Leadership is the power of one harnessing the power of many.

—John Maxwell

As a chapter officer, I found out very early that you can't act like a boss and just order people around. You have to learn how to be in charge; but at the same time, you have to work just as hard. It is impossible to do everything yourself or to solely rely on the officer team. Everyone has to get involved and help out with the planning and execution of activities. My chance to test this philosophy came when I led a committee for the first time.

Being an FFA chapter officer as a sophomore meant that I would be leading and directing others who were older and more experienced than I was. I was appointed chair of the sweatshirt committee. In our chapter the sweatshirt committee is a big deal. The sweatshirts that the committee designs are worn by most of our members, and the sweatshirts are a highly visible and effective public relations and recruiting tool for our chapter.

At first it was difficult for me to adjust to leading the upperclassmen, because I was so used to them leading me. My fears were eased and my confidence grew when I realized that I didn't have to do everything myself. During the first meeting, I realized that each member had talents and abilities to contribute that would be vital to our committee's success. As a result, I learned how to pull everyone's talents together, and we ended up with one of the most popular pieces of apparel that the FFA chapter had ever made.

Now, as a junior, I am continuing to develop my leadership skills. I have greater confidence in my own abilities and talents, but I will never forget the importance of pulling together the ideas and talents of others. It can be extremely difficult to accomplish personal and chapter goals if you are not open to the ideas and contributions of others.

Robert Gannett,
South Central FFA

What additional skills have helped you to successfully lead a committee or organization?

PERSONAL REFLECTIONS

Write your favorite quote from this chapter in the space below:

_____
_____
_____
_____
_____
_____

Why is this quote especially meaningful to you?

_____
_____
_____
_____
_____
_____
_____

Create a personal acronym for the word *leadership*. Identify the qualities and characteristics that are exhibited by outstanding leaders.

L _____
E _____
A _____
D _____
E _____
R _____
S _____
H _____
I _____
P _____

How can you be a leader today?

_____
_____
_____
_____
_____
_____

Chapter 6

Visiting the Museum

Taking Time to Learn and Grow

All of the top achievers I know are lifelong learners ... looking for new skills, insights, and ideas. If they're not learning, they're not growing ... not moving toward excellence.

—Denis Waitley

Your name may be on a diploma or degree, but the goal of realizing success and becoming a top achiever requires lifelong learning. The learning process should be evident in both your career and personal life, and it should not be limited to formalized instruction in a classroom or seminar setting. Learning can even occur while you are on vacation.

One of my favorite stops on our trip out west was Cody, Wyoming. In addition to being known as the Rodeo Capital of the World, Cody is home to the museum built in honor of its namesake, Buffalo Bill Cody, the famed trapper, trader, frontiersman, and actor. The large complex actually consists of five separate museums. The exhibits in the Buffalo Bill Museum represent both the personal and public lives of William Frederick "Buffalo Bill" Cody, and his story is shared in the context of the history and myth of the American West. The Whitney Gallery contains an outstanding collection of artwork depicting the American West from the early nineteenth century to today. The Plains Indian Museum features one of the country's largest collections of Plains Indian art and artifacts. The Cody Firearms Museum has the world's most comprehensive collection of American arms and includes an impressive collection of prized wildlife mounts from hunting expeditions. The exhibits in the Draper Museum of Natural History are designed to help visitors learn more about the greater Yellowstone ecosystem and its natural resources and animal habitats. With so much to see, it is easy to understand why we spent two days visiting the museum.

The artwork throughout the museum complex is truly phenomenal. I was especially moved by an oil painting in the Whitney Gallery that depicted Native Americans hunting buffalo, because it greatly challenged some of my preconceived ideas. Based on what I remembered from elementary school social studies, I had always envisioned buffalo hunts taking place on the open plains, with a warrior on horseback riding alongside a buffalo with his long-handled spear drawn in anticipation of the kill. I also assumed the warrior brought the buffalo back to the teepee so that the women could begin their work of preserving and curing the meat and tanning the hides. But this particular oil painting told a completely different story. Many warriors were driving large herds of buffalo over cliffs, and the women and children were already at the bottom, beginning their work. My understanding of the danger experienced and the sheer volume of work involved for both the men and women was radically altered.

As your life journey continues, plan to have similar museum experiences along the way. Search for opportunities that will challenge your preconceived ideas and cause you to see information from new perspectives. Work to improve your skills, and look for ways to rejuvenate your interests.

THE NEED FOR PERSONAL GROWTH

In the classic book *The 7 Habits of Highly Effective People*, Stephen Covey describes the seventh habit as "Sharpening the Saw." He opens the chapter about this habit with a story about a man who had been trying to saw down a tree for more than five hours. An onlooker asks him why he doesn't take a break for a few minutes, so he can sharpen his saw. The man replies: "I'm too busy sawing!"[1]

Whether we are busy or not, many individuals neglect to recognize the importance of improving themselves physically, mentally, socially, and spiritually. Growth in these areas does indeed make us more highly effective. In the NIV (New International Version) Bible you will find the following written in Ecclesiastes 10:10: "If the ax is dull and its edge unsharpened, more strength is needed, but skill will bring success." Said another way, skill may enable you to cut with a dull ax, but you sure will have to work a lot harder and use more strength than had you just sharpened the saw first.

Change in inevitable. Everybody has to deal with it. On the other hand, growth is optional. You can choose to grow or fight against impending change. But remember this: Staying where you are, as you are, is a prescription for becoming obsolete. Just ask the unsharpened saw that eventually gets discarded. In order to develop the skills that bring success, you must make a conscious choice to pursue personal growth. The degrees earned, experiences gained, awards received, or financial resources accumulated will not determine whether or not you reach your potential. What makes the greatest difference is your commitment to personal growth.

DISCOVER YOUR STRENGTHS

One of the fundamental principles of personal development is that your weakest skill area will limit your ability to take advantage of your strongest skill area. One of the traditional responsibilities of supervisors, teachers/professors, and even medical professionals is to evaluate your personal performance. Guided by a rubric, checklist, or some other type of test, these individuals are prepared to tell you how to change your work performance, raise your grade, or increase your health.

Traditionally, the emphasis is placed on what must be improved, but thanks to the work of the late Donald Clifton, the father of strengths psychology, a different philosophy is being considered by those who strive for peak performance. While weaknesses and deficiencies do need to be identified and managed, Clifton suggests that greater potential for growth and skill improvement occurs when individuals invest energy into developing their strengths instead.

So what are strengths? Unlike the skills or knowledge that you can acquire through education, your brain is wired with certain talents at birth. Talents are things that come naturally and easily for you. Think of your talents as special gifts that make you unique from others. The key to building your strengths is to identify your dominant talents and refine them through practice.

There are many tests you can take to help assess your personal strengths. I have personally used and would recommend the *StrengthsFinder* test. In 1998, while working for the Gallup Organization, Donald Clifton assembled a team of scientists to develop a common language for defining strengths. After more than two million talent-based interviews were conducted with successful executives, salespeople, customer service representatives, teachers, doctors, lawyers, students, nurses, and several other professions, Clifton and his team identified more than four hundred themes of talent.

The list was condensed to the following thirty-four signature themes that are most prevalent among top achievers and leaders: achiever, activator, adaptability, analytical, arranger, belief, command, communication, competition, connectedness, consistency, contest, deliberative, developer, discipline, empathy, focus, futuristic, harmony, ideation, include, individualization, input, intellection, learner, maximize, positivity, relator, responsibility, restorative, self-assurance, significance, strategic, and woo (the ability to win others over).

Clifton and Tom Rath continued their work for the Gallup Organization and developed the online inventory called *StrengthsFinder*, which assists people in discovering their talents. The key code for accessing the initial version of the online assessment was included with the 2001 release of the bestselling management book *Now, Discover Your Strengths.* Today you can also access the assessment with a key code from the book *StrengthsFinder 2.0.*[2] The Gallup Organization has also developed a *StrengthsQuest* program for college students. For more information about the program visit their Web site: http://www.strengthsquest.com.

Knowing your core strengths will enable you to select a rewarding career path based on your unique combination of talents. You will find yourself happiest working in a career that allows you to take advantage of your strengths on a daily basis. I suggest you complete at least one strengths assessment in order to help identify your personal talents. Working from your strengths will help you to:

- Be much more productive
- Achieve better results
- Contribute more value to your company or organization
- Enjoy your work
- Experience greater fulfillment
- Realize your potential

CREATE A PERSONAL DEVELOPMENT PLAN

An essential strategy for developing your talents to full potential is to create a personal development plan. As CEO of your life, you need to know where you want to be in the future. With that destination in mind, create a plan that identifies the skills, experiences, and credentials required to get there. The time to prepare is now, because you want to be ready when the next door of opportunity opens.

Even though you may realize that continual learning is important, you may still struggle with making time for personal development. Successful people frequently borrow the often quoted phrase from Larry the Cable Guy and say, "Just get 'r done."

On a more serious note, Henry Ford once said, "It's been my observation that most successful people get ahead during the time other people waste." What time have you been wasting that could be put to better use?

Learning something every day is the essence of being a continual learner. Make it a goal to read at least one book each month related to a strength theme. Try reading two Internet or journal articles each week. Books on tape and recordings from motivational speakers are also great resources for those who spend time commuting each day. How you choose to learn isn't as important as the effort you put forth. You will experience greater results if you follow through on a scheduled routine than if you put it off and periodically try to catch up.

USING MENTORS AS A RESOURCE

According to Brian Tracy, a successful businessman and professional speaker, "No one lives long enough to learn everything they need to learn starting from scratch. To be successful, we absolutely, positively have to find people who have already paid the price to learn the things that we need to learn to achieve our goals." Mentors are individuals who can jump-start our learning curves.

Make a list of individuals who have triumphed over the specific challenges you face. Some of the easiest ways to research people who have been successful in your area of interest are to read industry magazines, search the Internet, and network with college faculty or experienced professionals in your field of interest. Look for mentors who have the kind of well-rounded experience you need to tackle your goal, and ask them to teach you what you need to know in order to succeed.

When approached, some potential mentors will say no while others will say yes. Keep asking until you find someone who is willing to assist you. I appreciate the analogy that Dondi Scumaci makes in her book, *Designed for Success*. She writes, *"The most valuable, vital employees are rivers, not reservoirs, of information. They do not collect and store knowledge. They allow knowledge to flow through them by coaching and mentoring others. They give the information away."*[3] Many successful people do indeed enjoy sharing with others what they have learned.

For a mentoring relationship to be productive, you must take the initiative and have a clear understanding of the outcomes you desire. Be up-front about what you are hoping to learn. Articulate the specific challenges you are facing. Explain the projects you are working on as well as the feedback you have received. Describe where you want to be in one, five, and ten years. But remember this—mentors do not like to have their time wasted. After you seek out their advice, be sure to follow it.

Mentors are a great resource for helping you to see possibilities. They can encourage you to try new approaches, and they can help push you out of a comfort zone. Mentors often offer new perspectives, and they challenge you to see old situations in new ways. They guide you in learning from mistakes, and they will be great encouragers when you celebrate success.

SUMMING IT UP

- The learning process should be evident in both your career and personal life, and it is not limited to formalized instruction in a classroom or seminar setting.

- You should search for opportunities that will challenge your preconceived ideas and cause you to see information from new perspectives. Work to improve your skills, and look for ways to rejuvenate your interests.

- Growth is optional. But remember this: Staying where you are, as you are, is a prescription for becoming obsolete.

- You realize greater potential for growth and skill improvement when you invest energy into developing your strengths instead of focusing on your weaknesses.

- The key to building strengths is to identify your dominant talents and refine them with practice.

- Knowing your core strengths will enable you to select a rewarding career path based on your unique combination of talents.

- Mentors are individuals who can jump-start your learning curve. For a mentoring relationship to be productive, you must take initiative and have a clear understanding of the outcome you desire.

The following quote from John Maxwell helps to summarize the importance of personal development: *"Growth today is an investment for tomorrow. If you don't make growth your responsibility, it will never happen."* Make it your goal to learn something new every day, and keep yourself open to all the museum experiences life has to offer.

WORDS OF WISDOM

1. Move out of your comfort zone. You can only grow if you are willing to feel awkward and uncomfortable when you try something new.

    —Brian Tracy

2. Unless you do something beyond what you've already mastered, you will never grow.

    —Ralph Waldo Emerson

3. Always dream and shoot higher than you know you can do. Don't bother just to be better than your contemporaries or predecessors. Try to be better than yourself.

    —William Faulkner

4. We grow faster and stronger by learning from each other and being accountable to each other.

    —Rick Warren

5. Life is a gift, and it offers us the privilege, opportunity, and responsibility to give something back by becoming more.

    —Tony Robbins

6.   Never become so much of an expert that you stop gaining expertise. View life as a continuous learning experience.

—Denis Waitley

7.   We can't become what we need to be by remaining what we are.

—Oprah Winfrey

8.   Building a better you is the first step to building a better America.

—Zig Ziglar

9.   One's mind, once stretched by a new idea, never regains its original dimensions.

—Oliver Wendell Holmes

10.   Never be satisfied. Work constantly to improve. Perfection is a goal that can never be reached, but it must be the objective.

—John Wooden

11.   Leadership and learning are indispensable to each other.

—John F. Kennedy

12.   I do not think much of a man who is not wiser today than he was yesterday.

—Abraham Lincoln

13.   If you wish to achieve worthwhile things in your personal and career life, you must become a worthwhile person in your own self-development.

—Brian Tracy

14.   Without continual growth and progress, such words as improvement, achievement, and success have no meaning.

—Benjamin Franklin

15.   You cannot expect to achieve new goals or move beyond your present circumstances unless you change.

—Les Brown

16. Don't worry about being better than someone else, but never cease trying to be the best you can become.

—John Wooden

17. Learn from yesterday, live for today, hope for tomorrow. The important thing is not to stop questioning.

—Albert Einstein

18. Have a passion to learn. The more you discover about life and the world, the more complete and fulfilled you'll become. Make it a lifelong process.

—Hal Urban

19. If you desire to change yourself, then start with your mind. Believe you can improve, that you can change into the person you desire to be.

—John Maxwell

20. Become addicted to constant and never-ending self improvement.

—Anthony J. D'Angelo

21.   Minds are like parachutes; they work best when open.

—Lord Thomas Dewar

22.   To make something out of yourself, you need to be willing to change, for without change there can be no growth.

—John Maxwell

23.   You must take personal responsibility. You cannot change the circumstance, the seasons, or the wind, but you can change yourself. That is something you have charge of.

—Jim Rohn

24.   When you improve a little each day, eventually big things occur... seek the small improvement one day at a time.

—John Wooden

25.   There is no way of improving anything, until one has learned how to improve one's self.

—Phyllis Bottome

26.   The more you read, the more things you will know. The more you learn, the more places you'll go.

—Dr. Seuss

27.   The path to success lies in the realization that there is always more to learn.

—John Wooden

28.   An open mind is the beginning of self-discovery and growth. We can't learn anything new until we can admit that we don't already know everything.

—Erwin G. Hall

29.   Anyone who stops learning is old, whether at twenty or eighty. Anyone who keeps learning stays young. The greatest thing in life is to keep your mind young.

—Henry Ford

30.   When an archer misses the mark, he turns and looks for the fault within himself. Failure to hit the bull's-eye is never the fault of the target. To improve your aim, improve yourself.

—Gilbert Arland

A LESSON FROM A STORY

Self-improvement never ends—it is a lifelong process.

—Fran Hewitt

For me, self-improvement plays a key role in achieving success—not only in FFA but in life in general. Contests have been a great way for me to see my progress and track my improvement. In addition to being an FFA member, I am also a cross-country runner. Let's say, for example, that I run a five-kilometer race in seventeen minutes and thirty seconds. That is a good time, but I'm not going to say I am satisfied with that time and not train anymore. No way! I want to train and beat that time at our next meet, so I'm going to bust my butt to do it.

I am also our FFA chapter's student advisor, and serving as an officer is where I really learned character skills. With this position, I took on way more responsibility then I ever had before. I learned to make myself a better role model for others. The one person who has played a key role in my personal development has been my chapter advisor, Miss Chenevey. She has taught me important skills that I will use throughout life. Miss Chenevey challenges students to meet the high standards she sets. Sometimes it seems that she is just being tough on people, but I have come to realize that the hard work makes us better.

So far, I've completed three years in the FFA program, and I can say it's one of the best decisions I have ever made. I can take all the leadership skills I learn in FFA and use them in other activities, whether it be cross-country, track, 4-H, or student council. I am always looking to improve and make myself better. Don't be satisfied with being mediocre. You've got to want something more and challenge yourself to go after it. That's what my FFA experience has instilled in me, and I hope it's done the same for other members across the nation.

Jared Zollars,
West Holmes FFA

How are you challenging yourself to improve?

PERSONAL REFLECTIONS

Write your favorite quote from this chapter in the space below:

_____
_____
_____
_____
_____
_____

Why is this quote especially meaningful to you?

_____
_____
_____
_____
_____
_____
_____
_____

Review the Notes section at the end of this book. Select two titles you would like investigate further.

_____
_____
_____
_____
_____

Generate a list of four possible mentors, and describe what kind of help you would ask of them.

_____
_____
_____
_____
_____
_____
_____

Chapter 7

Stopping at the Service Station

Finding Opportunities to Volunteer

Life's most persistent urgent question is: What are you doing for others?

—Martin Luther King, Jr.

I have driven as far north as Toronto, Canada; as far south as Marco Island, Florida; as far east as Norfolk, Virginia; and as far west as Las Vegas, Nevada. I have logged thousands of miles commuting to college, driving for work, traveling on vacations, going shopping, pursuing recreational activities, and chauffeuring children. Needless to say, I've stopped at many gas stations throughout the years.

Gas stations were once commonly called service stations, because consumers were given a choice between self-serve and full-serve fuel pumps. As the name implies, the self-serve pump gave drivers the option of filling their own gas tanks, just as we do today.

With full service, however, the station attendant would fill the tank and wash your vehicle's windows, both front and back, before asking you to pop the hood so that he could check the oil and wiper fluid levels. The station had a full-service garage on site, with mechanics available to tune your vehicle's engine, change the oil, and rotate and balance the tires. The garage provided services that most drivers didn't do themselves. Gas stations of years past provide a good illustration that service is all about meeting a need while helping others.

STUDENTS LEARN THROUGH SERVICE

Today's teens are participating in service opportunities as part of their educational experiences in ever-increasing numbers. Statistics from the Corporation for National and Community Service indicate that more than 1.47 million students participated in service learning activities in 2005.[1] Some schools have made community service a requirement for graduation. Even colleges and universities are asking prospective students to describe their volunteer efforts on enrollment applications.

As defined by the National Service Learning Clearinghouse, service learning is a teaching and learning strategy that integrates meaningful community service with instruction and reflection to enrich the learning experience, teach civic responsibility, and strengthen communities.[2]

Schools are also providing additional community service opportunities through extra-curricular organizations and by awarding course credit for volunteerism. The service learning movement strives to instill in youth a passion for lifelong service and volunteerism.

PERSONAL BENEFITS OF VOLUNTEERING

Whether it is important for you to solve a community problem, advance a worthy cause, or develop as a person, volunteering offers many benefits to those who give their time and talents. Volunteering can help you:

Build a community: By addressing issues of concern, you, the volunteer, help make your community a better place for everyone. You will truly feel connected to others. While it is true that no one person can solve all the world's problems, you can make an enormous impact in your community and improve the little corner of the world where you live.

- *Fulfill a sense of purpose:* At its core, volunteering is about giving your time, energy, and skills freely. Your involvement is a testimony of your concern for others and commitment to a cause. By showing people what you are passionate about, you may inspire them to adopt an attitude of service too.
- *Learn or develop a new skill:* Volunteering for a program that is completely different from your studies or career focus enables you to gain a new skill set.
- *Explore new interests and hobbies:* Sometimes we get locked into the "rat race" of life, and volunteering can provide an escape to pursue new interests and hobbies. Volunteering can be fun, relaxing, and energizing.
- *Meet diverse groups of people:* Volunteering brings together people from all backgrounds and walks of life, and it offers an incredible opportunity to develop lasting personal and professional relationships. Networking is an exciting benefit of

volunteering. You never know who you will meet and what impact this could have on your life.

- *Make a difference in someone's life*: Mother Teresa once said, "If you can't feed a hundred people, then feed just one." Volunteer efforts don't only involve the masses. Organizations such as Big Brothers and Big Sisters provide mentoring opportunities that enable you to make a huge difference in an individual's life.
- *Give back*: One of the most common reasons people volunteer is to give back to society. Sharing your skills and talent provides nonprofit organizations with talent they could not normally afford to hire. Not only do you reap the benefit of making new contacts, but you feel good about contributing.
- *Pay forward*: In the true spirit of volunteerism, paying forward encourages you to look beyond yourself by doing something that will make the journey easier for someone yet to come. Your efforts may help reduce obstacles or eliminate barriers for the next generation.

IDENTIFYING YOUR KEY INTERESTS AND SKILLS FOR VOLUNTEERING

The interests and skills you bring to volunteering may be the same ones related to work, hobbies, and other interests. Here are some examples:

- If you like animals, you may enjoy helping out at a local animal shelter. Most shelters rely on volunteers to keep the cats and dogs exercised.
- If you are interested in politics, volunteering to help with a campaign is a great way to find out how the process works from a new perspective.
- Knowing a friend or relative who has a medical condition may inspire you to donate your time to an organization that raises money for research or offers assistance to people with an illness.
- Maybe you have excellent public-speaking skills that you could use as an advocate for a cause that you care about.
- Some people choose volunteer opportunities that will enable them to use skills that are not related to their work or career. For instance, if you have a desk job, but want to spend more time outdoors, you might consider volunteering to clean up a city park or help plant a community garden.
- Do you enjoy playing the piano or other musical instrument? You could volunteer to play at a retirement community or nursing care facility on a regular basis, or you could also consider accompanying a church or community choir.

Keep in mind that one of the most valuable assets you can bring to any volunteer effort is compassion. Have an open mind and open heart. Be flexible and willing to do whatever is needed. Maintain a positive attitude, and share your enthusiasm. These attributes will make you a valued addition to any volunteer team.

FINDING OPPORTUNITIES TO SERVE

The Internet is a great place to begin researching more about volunteering. There are numerous sites to help you search for service opportunities by location, skills needed, age group you would prefer to work with, dates you are available to serve, and areas of interests. Begin by exploring these Web sites:

> www.volunteermatch.org
> www.idealist.org
> www.americorps.gov
> www.1-800-volunteer.org
> www.liveunited.org
> www.networkforgood.org/volunteer/
> www.pointsoflight.org

Be sure to also check the volunteer listings in your local telephone directory. Call or visit local organizations that are in need of volunteer help. Local opportunities might include:

- Church-sponsored outreach programs
- Community theaters and museums
- Retirement centers and senior housing complexes
- Crisis pregnancy centers
- Meals on Wheels and community food pantries
- Youth sports teams
- School tutoring and enrichment programs
- Shelters for the homeless or victims of domestic abuse

Whether due to lack of transportation, time constraints, a disability, or other reasons, many people prefer to volunteer using their phone or computers from home. The Points of Light Institute is just one example of an organization that maintains a national database of community-based volunteer centers that can use your "virtual" assistance. Regardless of how you choose to volunteer, carefully consider the commitment you are asked to make. Once you start, others will begin to depend upon you.

MAKING A COMMITMENT OF TIME

As pastor Rick Warren says, "Your time is your life. That is why the greatest gift you can give someone is your time." After discovering what interests you, decide how much time you want to spend volunteering. Give serious consideration to your schedule. Most organizations want volunteers to commit to a set amount of time every week or two, but many large organizations—especially those related to the environment or finding cures for diseases—have periodic day-long service and fund-raising activities.

Offering your time in service to others is a commitment that should not be made lightly. Efforts that appear to be small or infrequent do add up. Actress and comedienne Whoopi Goldberg put the contribution of time into perspective when she said, "If every American donated five hours a week, it would equal the labor of twenty million full-time volunteers."

SUMMING IT UP

- As defined by the National Service Learning Clearinghouse, service learning is a teaching and learning strategy that integrates meaningful community service with instruction and reflection to enrich the learning experience, teach civic responsibility, and strengthen communities.

- Volunteering can help you: build a community, fulfill a sense of purpose, learn or develop a new skill, explore new interests and hobbies, meet diverse groups of people, make a difference in someone's life, and give back to your community.

- The interests and skills you bring to volunteering may be the same ones related to work, hobbies, and other interests.

- Keep in mind that the most valuable assets you can bring to any volunteer effort are compassion, an open mind and heart, the flexibility and willingness to do whatever is needed, and a positive and enthusiastic attitude.

- The Internet can be a great place to learn more about volunteering. Be sure to also check the volunteer listings in your local telephone directory.

- Whether due to lack of transportation, time constraints, a disability, or other reasons, many people prefer to volunteer from home using their phone or computer.

- Offering your time in service to others is a commitment you should not make lightly.

Entertainer Danny Thomas made a profound statement when he said, "All of us are born for a reason, but all of us don't discover why. Success in life has nothing to do with what you gain in life or accomplish for yourself. It's what you do for others." Search for your unique stations of service throughout your life journey.

WORDS OF WISDOM

1. The purpose of human life is to serve and to show compassion and the will to help others.

    —Albert Schweitzer

2. Only those who have learned the power of sincere and selfless contribution experience life's deepest joy: true fulfillment.

    —Tony Robbins

3. It is the task of a good man to help those in misfortune.

    —Sophocles

4. The sole meaning of life is to serve humanity.

    —Leo Tolstoy

5. You can't live a perfect day without doing something for someone who will never be able to repay you.

    —John Wooden

6. My fellow Americans, ask not what your country can do for you; ask what you can do for your country.

    —John F. Kennedy

7. Service is the pathway to real significance.

    —Rick Warren

8. One of the secrets to living a fulfilled life is shifting your focus from acquiring material success to being of service to others.

    —Fran Hewitt

9. Balance, peace, and joy are the fruit of a successful life. It starts with recognizing your talents and finding ways to serve others by using them.

    —Thomas Kinkade

10. Successful people are always looking for opportunities to help others. Unsuccessful people are always asking, "What's in it for me?"

    —Brian Tracy

11.   Remember that the happiest people are not those getting more, but those giving more.

—H. Jackson Brown, Jr.

12.   The greatest gift is a portion of thyself.

—Ralph Waldo Emerson

13.   We are not here merely to make a living. We are here to enrich the world.

—Woodrow Wilson

14.   The measure of a life, after all, is not its duration, but its donation.

—Corrie ten Boom

15.   I don't know what your destiny will be, but one thing I do know: the only ones among you who will be really happy are those who have sought and found how to serve.

—Albert Schweitzer

16. Some people give time, some money, some their skills and connection, some literally give their life's blood. But everyone has something to give.

—Barbara Bush

17. It's only when we unselfishly give, and are not looking out for just ourselves, that the best things in life come our way.

—Hal Urban

18. You have to sow before you can reap. You have to give before you can get.

—Robert Collier

19. We make a living by what we get; we make a life by what we give.

—Winston Churchill

20. Even if it's a little thing, do something for others—something for which you get no pay but the privilege of doing it.

—Albert Schweitzer

21.   It is more blessed to give than to receive.

—Acts 20:35

22.   Consciously or unconsciously, every one of us does render some service or other. If we cultivate the habit of doing this service deliberately, our desire for service will steadily grow stronger and will make not only our own happiness, but that of the world at large.

—Mahatma Gandhi

23.   The more you serve others, the more fulfilled your life will be.

—Dr. Bernie Siegel

24.   You give but little when you give of your possessions. It is when you give of yourself that you truly give.

—Kahlil Gibran

25.   It is inevitable that every seed of useful service you sow will multiply itself and come back to you in overwhelming abundance.

—Napoleon Hill

26.   The greatest levels of contentment and self-satisfaction are experienced by those who have found a way to serve others... It is a universal principle that you cannot serve others without it coming back multiplied to yourself.

—Jack Canfield

27.   For in giving freely without guarantee of return, you set into motion an irresistible momentum of goodness. When we give, everyone is a winner.

—John Marks Templeton

28.   You will find, as you look back upon your life, that the moments that stand out are the moments when you have done things for others.

—Henry Drummond

29.   I don't think you ever stop giving. I really don't. I think it's an ongoing process. And it's not just about being able to write a check. It's being able to touch somebody's life.

—Oprah Winfrey

30.   We make a living by what we get, but we make a life by what we give.

—Norman MacEwan

A LESSON FROM A STORY

Some people give time, some money, some their skills and connection—some literally give their life's blood. But everyone has something to give.

—Barbara Bush

As an active FFA member, you learn to strive to be your best, explore new ideas, and give to the community around you. You learn that life is about giving and making things better for others as well as yourself. With a little effort, you can make someone's day. When you give, you can make someone smile.

Over a year ago our chapter sponsored a tractor pull contest at Eastern High School. I wanted to become more active in FFA, so I volunteered my time to help with the event. I was shy, and I figured helping at the tractor pull would be a good behind-the-scenes role for me. My participation gave me a great memory, which I will keep forever. My volunteer service involved working at the concessions stand. I was very busy grilling burgers, taking orders, and selling soda. The crowd appreciated my efforts, and I wanted to do more.

I was rewarded for donating my time at the tractor pull. I felt a real sense of pride while participating in a school and community event, and I even learned how to drive a tractor. More importantly, I learned that when you give a few hours of service to others, it can really make a difference. I was part of a successful fund-raising project for our chapter. I have learned that life is rewarding when you give.

Jaimie Salisbury,
Eastern Brown FFA

How can you give the gift of your time?

PERSONAL REFLECTIONS

Write your favorite quote from this chapter in the space below:

_____
_____
_____
_____
_____
_____

Why is this quote especially meaningful to you?

_____
_____
_____
_____
_____
_____
_____
_____

Describe a community service activity in which you have been involved. How did others benefit? How did you personally benefit?

_____
_____
_____
_____
_____
_____
_____
_____

Explore a Web site cited in this chapter that helps link volunteers with service opportunities. What did you find that interests you?

_____
_____
_____
_____
_____
_____

Chapter 8

Slowing Down for the Orange Barrels

Overcoming Challenges

Obstacles don't have to stop you. If you run into a wall, don't turn around and give up. Figure out how to climb it, go through it, or work around it.

—Michael Jordan

I do appreciate having MapQuest directions, but, unfortunately, they do not always alert you to the presence of the beautiful orange barrels that all too typically appear on the interstates throughout the summer months.

A trip that may be projected to take three and a half hours takes longer than four because road construction has traffic down to one lane for more than five miles. Consider the accident that closes both lanes of traffic for over an hour, and remember the detour that took you six miles out of your way because the bridge on the local highway was being repaired. Even icy road conditions in the middle of February can be considered an obstacle to overcome.

If you have been driving for a while, I am sure you have experienced your own share of obstacles and delays that have come between you and your destination. Even though these circumstances may drastically slow your progress, you will eventually arrive at your destination. Your life journey also has its share of construction zones, accidents, detours, and delays. It is not a question of *if* you are going to encounter obstacles and challenges. The critical issue is how you will handle them *when* you do.

EXPECT OBSTACLES AND CHALLENGES

For some people, obstacles are the signs that tell them something was not meant to be. Obstacles may mean that a goal should be abandoned. But, as this chapter's introductory quote from Michael Jordan points out, the mere existence of an obstacle isn't a good enough reason to quit. Meaningful goals will push you beyond your comfort zone, so it is only natural to expect challenges. Remember, however, that obstacles don't have to derail your efforts. You can use them to your advantage and grow stronger and wiser.

The idea of climbing a mountain seems to be the universal analogy for facing an obstacle or challenge. We have all been given the sage advice, "Don't make a mountain out of a molehill."

Consider the classic movie *The Sound of Music* and the song written by Rodgers and Hammerstein, "Climb Every Mountain." The movie, based on the true story of the von Trapp family, concludes with the family's escape from Nazi officers as they make their way over the Austrian mountains. For the von Trapp family, the mountain represents both a literal and figurative barrier to freedom.

A much more recent musical example of the mountain analogy comes from the movie *Back to Tennessee.* You don't have to be a Hannah Montana fan to appreciate the powerful message in the lyrics of the song "The Climb," recorded by Miley Cyrus. The chorus begins with Miley's reference to mountains, when she sings, "There's always going to be another mountain; I'm always going to want to make it move." What a frank admission that life's journey will always include challenges. If you are not familiar with the song, check out the lyrics on an Internet site such as http://www.lyrics.com.

At the beginning of the second verse, Miley sings, "The struggles I'm facing, the chances I'm taking, sometimes might knock me down, but, no, I'm not breaking." When facing obstacles, you do sometimes have to take risks. If the result isn't what you would have hoped, try a new approach. Take Miley's words to heart. You may get knocked down a few times, but you won't break.

Television commercials from the 1990s encouraged youth to "Be like Mike," so begin now by following Michael Jordan's advice. Reread his quote that opens this chapter. Decide how to climb over, go through, or work around your obstacles. And when you feel like you are ready to throw in the towel, remember the Energizer bunny and just keep going and going and going.

IDENTIFY THE ORANGE BARRELS

Take a moment, and identify the orange barrels in the construction zone of your life. What challenges are slowing you down and interfering with your journey? Fear is one of the most common obstacles that can keep people from achieving their goals. That is why it is so important to recognize that fear is simply your body's natural way of letting you know that you are out of your comfort zone.

Do you remember that sick-to-your-stomach feeling you had when you stood at the front of the classroom and gave your first book report in elementary school? Have you ever watched a horror movie such as *Friday the 13th*? If so, what made the hair stand up on the back of your neck or goose bumps appear on your arms? Both are classic examples of a biological reaction to fear.

Fear alerts you to possible danger and warns you to be cautious. A positive response to the fear of drowning would motivate you to carefully watch a young child at play on the beach. Fear of theft prompts you to lock doors and windows or even install a home security device, and fear of a potential collision causes you to drive defensively in order to avoid impact when another car swerves into your lane of traffic. It is normal to experience fear, and these examples show that there are positive ways to respond to fear.

The problem with fear arises when it prevents you from taking the necessary actions to achieve your goals. Les Brown, author and inspirational speaker, says, "Too many of us are not living our dreams, because we are living our fears." Are you guilty of letting fear limit your life experience?

Successful people understand that fear is something to be acknowledged, experienced, and overcome. They feel the fear but do what's required anyway. Fear can only slow you down if you let it. Almost everyone who achieves something of value has experienced fear and moved forward in spite of it.

Professional boxing manager Cus D'Amato once said, "The hero and the coward both feel exactly the same fear, only the hero confronts his fear and converts it into fire." Never lose sight of your goals, and allow them to provide the spark that turns your fear into fire.

SLOWED DOWN BY FAILURE

Failure is another one of those orange barrels that can drastically slow down your journey through life. Some people even allow failure to bring their journey to a grinding halt. But it isn't whether we fail that matters; it's how we fail that counts.

The difference between people who succeed in life and those who have difficulty creating success isn't found in the number of times they fail. It's found in the courage they have to try again. B. C. Forbes once said, "History has demonstrated that the most notable winners usually encountered heartbreaking obstacles before they triumphed. They finally won because they refused to become discouraged by their defeats."

Consider the examples of Thomas Edison and Abraham Lincoln. Both famous Americans experienced profound failure before achieving success. Edison made hundreds of attempts before successfully inventing the light bulb, and Lincoln was defeated in numerous political campaigns before being elected president of the United States.

There are three common mistakes people make regarding failure. The first one is trying too hard to avoid it. Some people play it so safe that they never take any risks. But risk is an important part of achieving success, and it is a key element of growth. Success doesn't come to you—you have to go out and find it. That requires sticking your neck out a bit and taking calculated, not careless, risks.

Another mistake people often make is to allow failure to defeat them. They get angry, frustrated, disappointed, and discouraged. Too often they give up completely and quit trying to accomplish their goals. The impact of failure depends greatly upon their attitude and choices.

The third common mistake people make is to jump up too quickly after they have been knocked down. Eagerness to achieve success may cause a person to take action again before reflecting upon what caused the setback. Soichiro Honda, founder of Honda Motors, once said, "Many people dream of success. To me, success can be achieved only through repeated failure and introspection." Failure can be one of life's greatest teachers, but you must be willing to take time and learn from it before going back to work on your goal.

LEARNING FROM FAILURE

If you are not continually learning from your mistakes, then you are likely to repeat them over and over again. Consider the following lessons of failure:

- *Change*: Failure teaches you to revise your course of action, and it gives you the opportunity to try a new approach. President John F. Kennedy once said, "There are risks and costs to a program of action, but they are far less than the long-range risks and costs of comfortable inaction." Once you know what won't work, change your game plan and try something different.
- *Humility*: Failure confronts you with your limitations and makes you realize that you are not invincible. All of us fail. The only person who avoids failure altogether is someone who never leaves the driveway. But you can't make the journey if you never leave home.
- *Perseverance*: Failure asks whether you will quit or become more determined to reach your goals. As hotel executive Conrad Hilton says, "Successful people keep moving. They make mistakes, but they don't quit."
- *Personal Accountability*: Failure teaches you to assume responsibility for your actions. As coach John Wooden says, "You can stumble and fall, make errors and mistakes, but you are not

a failure until you start blaming others, including fate, for your results."

- *Progress*: Each time you experience failure or setback, remind yourself that you are one step closer to achieving your dream. Each time you run a race and fail to finish first, examine your progress. Success can be found in coming in fourth today when you remember that in last week's race you finished sixth with a slower time. Consider your progress regardless of the endeavor.

Linda Armstrong, mother of famed cyclist Lance Armstrong, offers the following challenge. "Make an obstacle an opportunity. Make a negative a positive. If you can't give 100 percent, you won't make it. Never quit!" Individuals who have difficulty achieving success usually tend to avoid and ignore their obstacles and challenges. Successful people accept them and work through them, even when sacrifice is required. It's the process of meeting obstacles head-on and looking for solutions that gives life meaning. Assess your orange barrels and keep moving.

SUMMING IT UP

- It is not a question of *if* you are going to encounter obstacles and challenges. The critical issue is how you will handle them *when* you do.

- Meaningful goals usually push you beyond your comfort zone, so it is only natural to expect challenges.

- Successful people understand that fear is something to be acknowledged, experienced, and overcome. They feel the fear but do what's required anyway.

- The problem with fear arises when it prevents you from taking the necessary actions to achieve your goals.

- Failure is another one of those orange barrels that can drastically slow down your journey through life.

- The three common mistakes people frequently make regarding failure include: trying too hard to avoid it, giving up on their goals, and not taking time to reflect and learn from failure.

- Failure teaches lessons regarding change, humility, perseverance, personal accountability, and progress.

- It's this process of meeting obstacles head-on and looking for solutions that gives life meaning.

The famous aviator Charles Lindbergh once said, "Success is not measured by what a man accomplishes, but by the opposition he has encountered, and the courage with which he has maintained the struggle against overwhelming odds." Get busy and move your mountains.

WORDS OF WISDOM

---

1. The greatest accomplishment is not in never falling, but in rising again after you fall.

    —Vince Lombardi

2. Entrepreneurs are simply those who understand that there is little difference between obstacle and opportunity and are able to turn both to their advantage.

    —Niccolo Machiavelli

3. I know God will not give me anything I can't handle. I just wish that He didn't trust me so much.

    —Mother Teresa

4. Stand up to your obstacles, and do something about them. You will find that they haven't half the strength you think they have.

    —Norman Vincent Peale

5. It is only because of problems that we grow mentally and spiritually.

    —M. Scott Peck

6.   Always remember that striving and struggle precede success, even in the dictionary.

—Sarah Ban Breathnach

7.   Develop success from failures. Discouragement and failure are two of the surest stepping stones to success.

—Dale Carnegie

8.   When everything seems to be going against you, remember that the airplane takes off against the wind, not with it.

—Henry Ford

9.   You measure the size of the accomplishment by the obstacles you had to overcome to reach your goals.

—Booker T. Washington

10.   For every failure, there's an alternative course of action. You just have to find it. When you come to a roadblock, take a detour.

—Mary Kay Ash

11.   Enthusiasm releases the drive to carry you over obstacles and
       adds significance to all you do.

                                            —Norman Vincent Peale

12.   Most things worth doing never go quite the way they were
       planned. The challenge is to ignore the distractions, overcome
       the obstacles, and stay focused on the goal.

                                            —Billy Cox

13.   It's important to develop a solution-oriented mind. Give yourself
       the opportunity to turn problems and adversity into something
       meaningful.

                                            Fran Hewitt

14.   The pessimist sees difficulty in every opportunity. The optimist
       sees the opportunity in every difficulty.

                                            —Winston Churchill

15.   We are like jewels, shaped with the hammer and chisel of
       adversity.

                                            —Rick Warren

16. Press on. Obstacles are seldom the same size tomorrow as they are today.

—Robert H. Schuller

17. Adversity can make us stronger, smarter, better, tougher. Blaming your troubles on bad luck makes you weaker. Most worthwhile things in the competitive world come wrapped in adversity.

—John Wooden

18. Character is built in times of adversity. We change and learn from life's painful lessons.

—Fran Hewitt

19. It's okay if you fall down, as long as you learn something as you get up.

—John Maxwell

20. Show me someone who has done something worthwhile, and I'll show you someone who has overcome adversity.

—Lou Holtz

21.   When defeat comes, accept it as a signal that your plans are not sound, rebuild those plans, and set sail once more toward your coveted goal.

—Napoleon Hill

22.   Only through experiences of trial and suffering can the soul be strengthened, vision cleared, ambition inspired, and success achieved.

—Helen Keller

23.   When passion and courage join forces, adversity cannot stop you.

—Les Hewitt

24.   Expect trouble as an inevitable part of life, and repeat to yourself the most comforting words of all: This, too, shall pass.

—Ann Landers

25.   If you're willing to accept failure and learn from it, if you're willing to consider failure as a blessing in disguise and bounce back, you've got the potential of harnessing one of the most powerful success forces.

—Joseph Sugarman

26.   Failure isn't failure unless you don't learn from it.

—Ronald Niednagel

27.   We all know that life comes with issues, challenges, disappointments, failures, and misfortunes. But I like to call all of those things the fertilizer that seeds need in order to grow to their fullest.

—Delatorro McNeal II

28.   Always believe there is a positive to be found in the negative.

—John Wooden

29.   Our real success in life will be largely determined by how well we deal with adversity: whether we run from it or face up to it, whether we shrink or grow from it, whether we surrender to it or triumph over it.

—Hal Urban

30.   That which does not destroy me makes me stronger.

—Friedrich Nietzsche

A LESSON FROM A STORY

If you can't stand the heat, get out of the kitchen.

—Harry S. Truman

Born and raised in a smaller version of the concrete jungle, I grew up in a close, quiet neighborhood in the midst of Akron, Ohio. Dirt was a major problem for me, and I couldn't tell you the difference between a beef cow and a dairy cow. They were all the same to me—large smelly animals that pretty much used the world as their personal toilet. So when my mom took a construction job in Cincinnati and moved us four and a half hours south to rural Brown County, I had quite a major culture shock.

When the first day of school arrived, I found my new surroundings a bit foreign. The school was so small and full of surprises. I was planning my schedule for the year, and I came across a class called Agriculture Production I. Having a desire to learn more about the rural area, I decided to sign up for the class as an alternative to study hall. I had absolutely no intention of getting involved in an extracurricular organization. I just wanted to learn a little and move on to other things, but the class really drew me in.

For the first two years, my city roots provided much entertainment for the agriculture department. Everything about me was city, and I was the girl in Goth pants. I even cringed at the sight of dirt. But I soon discovered that if I was going to survive, I was going to have to make a few changes. Slowly I eased into a culture that was completely unlike the familiar and solitary life I had known in the city.

When I joined FFA I surrounded myself with a team. I have learned so much. I now know that dairy cows are not anorexic and that beef cows provide the best eating. I even got into tractor pulling and took some shop classes where I had to force myself to get really dirty. But my advisor quickly pointed out, "That's what they invented soap for." I've challenged myself to try new activities, even if I thought I might not like them, without complaining. Complaining gets on everyone's nerves, and no one really wants to hear it.

If I had complained instead of giving myself the chance to learn and grow through FFA, I would not be where I am now. Who would have known that I would show beef cows, judge dairy cows, and earn my State FFA Degree? Thanks to those shop classes, I am now planning to become a certified welder.

I have come a long way from where I started, all because I pushed forward and overcame a major life change without complaining. President

Truman would be pleased to know that the kitchen wasn't too hot for me, after all.

Brittani Whitson,
Eastern FFA

How does your attitude influence the way you deal with challenges?

PERSONAL REFLECTIONS

Write your favorite quote from this chapter in the space below:

_____
_____
_____
_____
_____

Why is this quote especially meaningful to you?

_____
_____
_____
_____
_____
_____
_____

What orange barrels and challenges are slowing you down and interfering with your efforts to achieve a goal? What are you doing to remove or work around them?

_____
_____
_____
_____
_____
_____
_____
_____

Identify a situation in which you experienced failure. What lessons did you learn?

_____
_____
_____
_____
_____
_____
_____

Chapter 9

Staying the Course

Hanging Tough with Perseverance

Consider it pure joy, my brothers, whenever you face trials of many kinds, because you know that the testing of your faith develops perseverance. Perseverance must finish its work, so that you may be mature and complete, not lacking anything.

—James 1:2–4, NIV Bible

Orange construction barrels can present quite a dilemma for a traveler. The length of the construction zone, the time of day, your knowledge of the area, and the added stress of needing to be at a particular place by a certain time can all factor into how you decide to handle a delay. As the driver, you can choose to maintain your route and simply slow down, but, if you are familiar with the locale, you may opt to change your route and entirely avoid the orange construction barrels.

I don't know anyone who encounters highway construction and says, "I'm not in the mood to deal with this today, so I'm going back home." Giving up is simply not a productive option, and it is not a recommended strategy for our travel on the highway of life either. The New Testament book written by the disciple James points out that testing of our faith develops perseverance, and perseverance is required to complete any task or goal.

Much has been attributed to the value of perseverance. For example, Winston Churchill led Great Britain though World War II with his grim determination to never surrender or give up. On a humorous note, the preacher Charles Spurgeon once said, "The snail would never have made it on the ark, except through long perseverance!"

Even our pop culture recognizes that perseverance and persistence are essential for success. Many teens have grown up hearing the sage advice, "If at first you don't succeed, try, try again," as well as, "Winners never quit and quitters never win." And everyone is familiar with the wise old fable about the tortoise and the hare.

THE TORTOISE AND THE HARE

As the story goes, there once was a race between a tortoise and a hare. The hare is an animal of great speed, while the tortoise, on the other hand, is characterized as moving very slowly. The hare jumps out to an early lead and decides to take a nap under a shade tree before finishing the race. While the hare naps, the tortoise never stops "running" his race, and he crosses the finish line first. The perseverance of the tortoise was the determining factor for his victory over the speedy hare.

As a runner in the race of life, it is necessary for you to have perseverance in order to reach the finish line. Unfortunately, many people abandon the race due to lack of perseverance. They start out toward their goals with the speed and enthusiasm of the hare, but they burn out quickly when faced with obstacles and challenges. Many have stumbled and decided not to get up. Many become discouraged and stop running. But the individuals who make the conscious choice to persevere, even in the midst of difficulties and challenges, are the ones who successfully finish the race. Which are you, a tortoise or a hare?

WHAT DOES IT MEAN TO PERSEVERE?

According to *Webster's Pocket Dictionary and Thesaurus*, to persevere is defined as having the ability to persist in any purpose or idea; to strive in spite of difficulties or obstacles.[1] People who persevere are persistent, diligent, steadfast, constant, unswerving, untiring, and tenacious. Former president Calvin Coolidge spoke of the value of perseverance and persistence when he said the following:

> Nothing in the world can take the place of persistence. Talent will not; nothing is more common than unsuccessful men with talent. Genius will not; unrewarded genius is almost a proverb. Education will not; the world is full of educated derelicts. Persistence and determination alone are omnipotent. The slogan "Press On" has solved and always will solve the problems of the human race.

At its core, perseverance is the ability to maintain action regardless of your feelings. As President Coolidge said, you "press on," even when you feel like quitting.

When you work toward achieving a goal, your motivation will fluctuate. Sometimes you will feel motivated; sometimes you won't. Remember, however, that it is not the level of motivation that produces results, but rather your actions. Perseverance encourages you to take action even when you don't feel motivated to do so. As a result, your efforts get you closer to achieving your goal.

Individuals with high levels of perseverance will stick with their course of action not just when the going gets tough, but even when others tell them to stop. Single mindedness, self-belief, determination, dedication, and the unwillingness to give in are what distinguish people who do great things with their lives from those who let their dreams die with them. When you display perseverance you consider what others say, but you don't let others' ideas control or limit you. You remain committed to your goals.

From learning to walk to riding a bicycle, our childhood teaches us that failure only occurs when we stop trying. It is a lesson that many people need to revisit in their adulthood. Perseverance and failure cannot coexist. Failure happens when you quit. Perseverance, also referred to as "stick-to-itiveness" is fundamental for realizing success.

WHAT IT TAKES TO PERSEVERE

The degree to which you are willing to persevere may be tested daily. Consider the following five recommendations that can help you persevere:

- *Have faith.* Be confident in your abilities, while you search to understand the greater meaning of life. From a Christian perspective, that greater meaning comes from God. Years ago, I saw a poster at church that read, "Work as if everything depends on you, and pray as if everything depends on God." Reflect on the principles of your religious faith during times when you are tempted to give up.
- *Adopt a healthy lifestyle.* Energy and stamina are essential for maintaining focus, resilience, optimism, and self-confidence. Diet, exercise, and adequate time for sleep and relaxation should not be ignored.
- *Be independent of negative influences.* When you take a leap of faith and succeed, some people may be envious or fearful that you are leaving them behind. This may cause them to be critical of your goals and plans. Don't allow them to diminish your dream. When you become overly concerned about what others say or how they judge your actions, you can lose your drive to persevere. Keep your dreams and goals in focus.
- *Seek advice from the experts.* Why get discouraged with redesigning your own wheel from scratch? If you want to shorten the time needed for accomplishing your goals, make an

extra effort to learn from other people. Talk to those who have achieved success doing what you want to do, and learn from their mistakes.

- *Revise your goals as needed.* Should you always persist and never give up? Certainly not. It can be a painful mistake to confuse stubbornness with perseverance. You can waste much time, energy, and resources if you unwisely pursue a goal that cannot be achieved. Sometimes the best option is to make a critical assessment of your progress and make revisions to your goal before moving ahead.

DIG A LITTLE DEEPER

The Web site www.inspirationalstories.com provides the following example of why the need for perseverance is so important.

There's a story about the California gold rush that tells of two brothers who sold all they had and went prospecting for gold. They discovered a vein of the shining ore, staked a claim, and proceeded to get down to the serious business of getting the gold ore out of the mine.

All went well at first, but then a strange thing happened. The vein of gold ore disappeared! They had come to the end of the rainbow, and the pot of gold was no longer there. The brothers continued to pick away, but without success. Finally, they gave up in disgust. They sold their equipment and claim rights for a few hundred dollars and took the train back home.

The man who bought the claim hired an engineer to examine the rock strata of the mine. The engineer advised him to continue digging in the same spot where the former owners had left off. And three feet deeper, the new owner struck gold. With a little more persistence, the two brothers would have been millionaires themselves.[2]

I challenge you to make the story of the gold rush a personal analogy, and remember that there is gold in you, too. Do you need to dig three feet farther? Despite failure and disappointment, you can achieve success. With perseverance, you will be able to stay the course, develop your potential, and achieve your goals.

SUMMING IT UP

- Giving up is simply not a productive option, and it is not a recommended strategy for our travel on the highway of life, either.

- The individuals who make the conscious choice to persevere, even in the midst of difficulties and challenges, are the ones who successfully finish the race.

- Perseverance allows you to keep taking action even when you don't feel motivated to do so.

- Single mindedness, self-belief, determination, dedication, and the unwillingness to give in are what distinguish people who do great things with their lives from those who let their dreams die.

- Follow these recommendations to help yourself persevere:

  Have faith.
  Adopt a healthy lifestyle.
  Be independent of negative influences.
  Seek advice from the experts.
  Revise your goals as needed.

Perseverance is essential for achieving success. Thomas Edison made thousands of attempts before inventing the electric light bulb. When asked about his failures, he replied, "I haven't failed. I've identified ten thousand ways this doesn't work." By viewing his setbacks as learning experiences, Edison could persevere and ultimately achieve success with numerous inventions.

WORDS OF WISDOM

1. No matter how many times the media tells us that there's a "quick and easy" way to get anything we want, we need to remind ourselves that nothing worthwhile has ever been achieved without the three P's: perseverance, persistence, and patience.

    —Hal Urban

2. Many of life's failures are people who did not realize how close they were to success when they gave up.

    —Thomas Edison

3. The majority of men meet with failure because of their lack of persistence in creating new plans to take the place of those which fail.

    —Napoleon Hill

4. You may have to fight a battle more than once to win it.

    —Margaret Thatcher

5. Determination gives you the resolve to keep going in spite of the roadblocks that lay before you.

    —Denis Waitley

6. The person who makes a success of living is one who sees his goal steadily and aims for it unswervingly. That's dedication.

    —Cecil B. DeMille

7. The truth is, life is difficult. To overcome its challenges you must exercise and strengthen those muscles that produce tenacity, passion, and persistence.

    —Fran Hewitt

8. Patience and perseverance have a magical effect before which difficulties and obstacles vanish.

    —John Quincy Adams

9. When you get to the end of your rope, tie a knot and hang on.

    —Franklin D. Roosevelt

10. Most people who succeed in the face of seemingly impossible conditions are people who simply don't know how to quit.

    —Robert H. Schuller

11.   It takes hunger, tenacity, and commitment to see a dream through until it becomes reality.

—John Maxwell

12.   Persistence is probably the single most common quality of high achievers. They simply refuse to give up. The longer you hang in there, the greater the chance that something will happen in your favor.

—Jack Canfield

13.   Let me tell you the secret that has led me to my goal: my strength lies solely in my tenacity.

—Louis Pasteur

14.   Don't give up; it's the people who have the fortitude to keep trying even in the face of adversity who eventually find success.

—Debbie Macomber

15.   Energy and persistence conquer all things.

—Benjamin Franklin

16.   Our greatest weakness lies in giving up. The most certain way to succeed is always to try just one more time.

—Thomas Edison

17.   It's the constant and determined effort that breaks down all resistance and sweeps away all obstacles.

—Claude M. Bristol

18.   Desire is the key to motivation, but it's the determination and commitment to an unrelenting pursuit of your goal—a commitment to excellence—that will enable you to attain the success you seek.

—Mario Andretti

19.   Ambition is the path to success. Persistence is the vehicle you arrive in.

—William Eardley IV

20.   Most people who fail in their dream fail not from lack of ability but from a lack of commitment.

—Zig Ziglar

21.   Most of the important things in the world have been accomplished by people who have kept on trying when there seemed to be no hope at all.

—Dale Carnegie

22.   You never really lose until you quit trying.

—Mike Ditka

23.   Success is almost totally dependent upon drive and persistence. The extra energy required to make another effort or try another approach is the secret of winning.

—Denis Waitley

24.   Push yourself again and again. Don't give an inch until the final buzzer sounds.

—Larry Bird

25.   Remember that just the moment you say "I give up," someone else seeing the same situation is saying, "My, what a great opportunity."

—H. Jackson Brown, Jr.

26.   Never quit. It is the easiest cop-out in the world. Set a goal and don't quit until you attain it. When you do attain it, set another goal, and don't quit until you reach it.

—Paul "Bear" Bryant

27.   Most people give up just when they're about to achieve success. They quit on the one yard line. They give up at the last minute of the game one foot from a winning touchdown.

—H. Ross Perot

28.   Never consider the possibility of failure; as long as you persist, you will be successful.

—Brian Tracy

29.   Never give up on your dream... Perseverance is all important. If you don't have the desire and the belief in yourself to keep trying after you've been told you should quit, you'll never make it.

—Tawni O'Dell

30.   Effort only fully releases its reward after a person refuses to quit.

—Napoleon Hill

A LESSON FROM A STORY

I can accept failure, but I can't accept not trying.

—Michael Jordan

I joined the FFA in the fall of 2004. I wanted to take an easy class that would get me through the day. The class was easy, but I didn't think the agriculture program was for me. I was one of the students who didn't live on a farm. I didn't have much farming experience, but little did I know how that would change in the years to come.

At the end of my freshman year, I contemplated whether I should take a second year of agriculture. I really wasn't sure if I wanted to stick it out for another year. But I persevered, and I'm so glad I decided to stay involved.

New opportunities soon came my way. I completed my first livestock project, which was a swine project, and exhibited it at the county fair. Had I not stuck with agriculture and FFA, I would have missed out on a new experience.

After being an FFA member for four years, I have learned that perseverance is frequently rewarded. By working hard, remaining committed to my personal goals, and participating in chapter activities, I was able to receive both the State and American Degrees. I am greatly appreciative of the support and encouragement of my advisor, Luke Rhonemus. He helped me identify projects that really interested me and encouraged me to keep trying.

I have benefited from FFA in many ways. No other program at our school could have given me the guidance, knowledge, and skills I have gained in the past four years. I am confidently accepting another new project as an alumni member. I am raising my first crop project—an acre of sweet corn. At first I didn't think I would be able to do it, but my project is indeed a reality. I finally see myself as a real farmer for the first time in my life. How different the last five years would have been if I had not persevered. Thanks to my involvement as an FFA member, I have confidence to keep trying new things.

Sean Polhemus,
Eastern Brown FFA

When have you chosen to persevere instead of giving up?

PERSONAL REFLECTIONS

Write your favorite quote from this chapter in the space below:

_____
_____
_____
_____
_____
_____

Why is this quote especially meaningful to you?

_____
_____
_____
_____
_____
_____
_____
_____

Describe a personal situation that required perseverance in order for you to achieve success.

_____
_____
_____
_____
_____
_____
_____
_____

What enabled you to persevere?

_____
_____
_____
_____
_____
_____
_____

Chapter 10

Taking the Scenic Route

Expressing Appreciation through Gratitude

*Develop an attitude of gratitude, and give thanks for everything
that happens to you, knowing that every step forward is a step
toward achieving something bigger and better than your current
situation.*

—Brian Tracy

There are three main routes you can take from our home in rural southern
Ohio to Cincinnati. One route is a two-lane state highway that goes through
small towns and has numerous traffic lights and congested traffic that can
slow your progress.

Another route adds an additional five miles to your travel distance, but
the ease and convenience of driving on a four-lane highway with fewer
traffic lights makes this route more appealing.

The final route is a scenic highway that adds more than fifteen miles to
your total driving distance, but it is a beautiful route that meanders along
the Ohio River. While traveling the four-lane highway is generally the norm,
I do enjoy taking the scenic drive, especially during the summer. The water
skiers, and those who enjoy tubing, often provide an entertaining show. I
am grateful for the opportunity to relax and unwind as I watch the action
on the river.

How often do you opt to take the scenic route to reach your destination?
Too often on the journey of life, people choose to travel on the four-lane
highways and interstate routes while avoiding the scenic routes. They
get so caught up in being efficient and productive in order to achieve

success that they neglect to slow down and appreciate the blessings and enjoyment of the journey itself.

COUNT YOUR BLESSINGS

It is unfortunate that Thanksgiving is the only day on the calendar that reminds some people to pause and give thanks for their blessings. But you don't have to declare a national holiday and eat some turkey in order to recognize and celebrate your blessings.

There is really no reason why you can't do that every day of the year. Being thankful can become a way of life, if you begin one day at a time. Television talk show host Oprah Winfrey once said, "Be thankful for what you have; you'll end up having more. If you concentrate on what you don't have, you will never, ever have enough."

Over the years Oprah has been a proponent of keeping a daily gratitude journal. While some people choose to write paragraphs in a short story format, others opt to simply make a list of five things for which they are grateful each day. Test the premise of Oprah's quote. Challenge yourself to write daily in a gratitude journal, and see if you end up having more to be thankful for.

Make a commitment to yourself that you will write in your journal at least once a day. It doesn't have to take a long time. Even five minutes is better than nothing at all. If you have had a terrible day, it may take a bit longer, but you can be grateful for the small things, such as the chance to listen to more of your favorite music instead of fuming about the traffic that made you late for work or school.

Consider keeping the journal at your bedside, and write in it at the start of your day or before going to sleep at night. By writing something in your journal each day, you will more easily recognize the things you appreciate instead of taking them for granted. Focusing your mind on being grateful will soon replace your thoughts about the things you don't have.

Read your journal when you have an occasional bad day and be reminded about all that is right with life. Being thankful, if practiced regularly, becomes a habit. You will soon discover that appreciation is closely linked to fulfillment.

GRATITUDE AND WELL-BEING

Robert Emmons, Ph.D., is a noted psychology professor at the University of California, Davis. As one of the leading scholars in the positive psychology movement, his foremost interests lie in the psychology of gratitude and personal goals. His most recent research into the correlation of gratitude and happiness gives fascinating insight into the power of personal thought and attitude.

When interviewed about his newest book *Thanks!: How the New Science of Gratitude Can Make You Happier,* Emmons was asked if he was surprised by the research findings contained in his book. Here's his response:

> The effect seemed to be so immediate. When you start to grow gratitude in your life, the benefit seems to be so wide. It's not simply that you feel better or happier—although that's certainly legitimate—but, the fact is, there are interpersonal benefits. You feel more connected to others. You feel a greater sense of obligation to go out do something that's useful or beneficial. You sleep better. The benefits just seem limitless when you practice gratitude.[1]

Grateful people generally have more positive ways of coping with life's difficulties. They are more likely to seek support and assistance from other people, instead of labeling themselves as victims. Grateful people spend more time planning how to deal with problems, rather than avoiding them or blaming others for their difficulties. Thankfulness does wonders for the body and soul. When you focus on what is right, instead of what is wrong, your well-being improves considerably.

CHOOSE AN ATTITUDE OF GRATITUDE

If you want to make gratitude part of your daily life, you must choose to do so. Begin by searching for something to be grateful for in every experience. When something happens—either good or bad—pause for a moment, and choose how you want to feel about it.

Many people are in the habit of thinking negatively. They experience something difficult or painful and the situation sends them immediately into a negative state of mind. They fluctuate between feelings of anger, resentment, disappointment, or annoyance, while never understanding that they have the power to consciously choose a positive mind-set.

Do your best to find something positive about every situation. If you are used to looking at the negative side of each experience, this will be quite a challenge, but keep working at it until you can find at least one good thing about any situation. Part of this process involves seeing with new eyes. Stand back, change your perspective, and look for what is good. As Wayne Dyer says, "When you change the way you look at things, the things you look at change."

But don't try to fake it! If you have a flat tire on the highway, you can't mutter through gritted teeth, "I'm really grateful for this," over and over and expect good things to come from the situation. You really are *not* grateful for a flat tire!

Instead, find an aspect of the situation that you really *can* be grateful about. You might, for example, choose to feel grateful for the vacant lot that was nearby. You were able to pull off the road and safely change the tire without further incident. Regardless of what you come up with, be sure your feeling of gratitude is genuine.

Years ago, I was given a copy of the following poem. I share it with you because it helps to clearly explain why an attitude of gratitude is one of the fundamental principles for achieving success in life.

"Be Thankful"
—Author unknown

Be thankful that you don't already have everything you desire.
If you did, what would there be to look forward to?

Be thankful when you don't know something.
For it gives you the opportunity to learn.

Be thankful for the difficult times.
During those times you grow.

Be thankful for your limitations.
Because they give you opportunities for improvement.

Be thankful for each new challenge.
Because it will build your strength and character.

Be thankful for your mistakes.
They will teach you valuable lessons.

Be thankful when you're tired and weary.
It means you've made a difference.

It's easy to be thankful for the good things.
But a life of rich fulfillment comes to those who are also thankful for the setbacks.

Gratitude can turn a negative into a positive.
Find a way to be thankful for your troubles and they can become your blessings.

EXPRESS GRATITUDE TO OTHERS

The special people who enrich our lives every day are among some of our greatest blessings. We all know people who encourage, teach, bring out the best in us, and simply lift our spirits. Because of them we try harder, perform better, and experience life more fully.

One of the greatest gifts you can give is to acknowledge others with honest appreciation and gratitude. Noted sociologist William James once said, "The deepest principle in human nature is the craving to be appreciated." Studies show that appreciation for a job well done is more important to most people than money. Do you remember how you felt the last time someone acknowledged you?

Most likely it would be very easy for you to create a list of people you greatly appreciate. But when was the last time you expressed your gratitude to these individuals?

WHAT TO SAY

If you have taken a speech or communication class, you may have already learned how an *I message* can be used as an effective communication technique for resolving personal conflicts. *I messages* were originally studied by Dr. Haim Ginott, a noted psychologist, who found that statements starting with I tended to be less provocative or confrontational than those starting with you.[2] Instead of blaming others, the *I message* format guides you through communicating four critical components:

- stating a problem
- taking ownership of your feelings
- suggesting a change in behavior
- describing the desired outcome

The first attempts to practice the technique probably seem artificial and scripted, but with practice and repetition it becomes much easier to deliver an effective *I message*.

Most people have a rather extensive vocabulary for complaining and venting their anger, but they seem to get easily tongue-tied when it comes to expressing appreciation and thankfulness. If the *I message* works so well as a technique for conflict resolution, a similar communication model could be used to express thankfulness and appreciation. I call such statements *gratitude messages.*

Begin by stating the action that you appreciate. Be specific, and remind the other person what they did to make you thankful. Next, describe your feelings, and then include a description of the personal impact that resulted. Conclude by offering a simple thank you. Here are some examples:

- When I saw that the tools were put away in the garage I felt very thankful, because I can get easily frustrated when I'm in the middle of a project and can't find the tools I need. I appreciate the time you took to put everything away.
- When I received your phone call I felt so relieved and happy, because I had been worrying about how you might have been affected by the storm. I am so glad that you are okay. Thanks for calling.
- When I felt you put your arm around me at Uncle Bill's funeral, I felt so much love and comfort. I really needed the support, and I want to thank you for being there for me.

Just like with an *I message,* your first attempts at delivering a gratitude message may sound awkward. Keep reminding yourself of the old saying, "Practice makes perfect." In a matter of seconds, you can make someone else's day simply by expressing your gratitude. In fact, you make two people feel very good—the person you thank and yourself. What a great example of a win-win scenario.

Using technology can also make it easy to share your gratitude with others. E-mail and text messages can assist you with expressing gratitude if you are a little on the shy side. Better yet, a handwritten note that expresses your gratitude might be kept and treasured by the recipient for years.

SUMMING IT UP

- Gratitude starts with noticing the positive around you and acknowledging your blessings.

- Keep a daily gratitude journal. By writing something in your journal each day, you will create a mindset for recognizing the things you appreciate instead of taking them for granted.

- Thankfulness does wonders for the body and soul. When you focus on what is right, instead of what is wrong, your well-being improves considerably.

- Do your best to find something positive about every situation.

- One of the greatest gifts you can give is to acknowledge others with honest appreciation and gratitude.

- Begin a *gratitude message* by describing the action that you appreciate. Next, describe your feelings, and then include a description of the personal impact that resulted. Conclude by offering a simple thank you.

- In a matter of seconds, you can make someone else's day simply by expressing your gratitude. In fact, you make two people feel very good—the person you thank and yourself.

Heed the suggestion from the beginning of this chapter. Take time to slow down and enjoy the scenic route, so that you can recognize and appreciate all that you have to be thankful for. Make time to express your gratitude to others.

WORDS OF WISDOM

1.   To recognize and appreciate all of the blessings in our lives, we need to develop eyes that can see them. Cultivating an attitude of gratitude will have the greatest impact on your happiness.

—Fran Hewitt

2.   Persons thankful for little things are certain to be the ones with much to be thankful for.

—Frank Clark

3.   He is a wise man who does not grieve for the things which he has not, but rejoices for those which he has.

—Epictetus

4.   Look for things to appreciate in every situation. When you actively seek the positive, you become more appreciative and optimistic, which is a requirement for creating the life of your dreams. Look for the good.

—Jack Canfield

5.   We often take for granted the very things that most deserve our gratitude.

—Cynthia Ozick

6. The more you appreciate something, the more it tends to increase in your life.

    —M. J. Ryan

7. When you arise in the morning, give thanks for the morning light, for your life and strength. Give thanks for your food and the joy of living. If you see no reason for giving thanks, the fault lies with yourself.

    —Tecumseh, Shawnee chief

8. The more you praise and celebrate your life, the more there is in life to celebrate.

    —Oprah Winfrey

9. Appreciation can make a day, even change a life. Your willingness to put it into words is all that is necessary.

    —Margaret Cousins

10. We tend to forget that happiness doesn't come as a result of getting something we don't have, but rather of recognizing and appreciating what we do have.

    —Frederick Keonig

11.   How happy a person is depends upon the depth of his gratitude.

—John Miller

12.   Of all the attitudes we can acquire, surely the attitude of gratitude is the most important, and by far the most life-changing.

—Zig Ziglar

13.   You simply will not be the same person two months from now after consciously giving thanks each day for the abundance that exists in your life. And you will have set in motion an ancient spiritual law: The more you have and are grateful for, the more will be given you.

—Sarah Ban Breathnach

14.   As we express our gratitude, we must never forget that the highest appreciation is not to utter words, but to live by them.

—John F. Kennedy

15.   Gratitude is a quality similar to electricity: it must be produced and discharged and used up in order to exist at all.

—William Faulkner

16.   Train yourself never to put off the word or action for the expression gratitude.

—Albert Schweitzer

17.   I started out giving thanks for small things, and the more thankful I became, the more my bounty increased. That's because what you focus on expands, and when you focus on the goodness in your life, you create more of it.

—Oprah Winfrey

18.   If you want to turn your life around, try thankfulness. It will change your life mightily.

—Gerald Good

19.   Reflect each day on all you have to be grateful for, and you will receive more to be grateful for.

—Chuck Danes

20.   Feeling gratitude and not expressing it is like wrapping a present and not giving it.

—William Arthur Ward

21.   At times our own light goes out and is rekindled by a spark from another person. Each of us has cause to think with deep gratitude of those who have lighted the flame within us.

—Albert Schweitzer

22.   Silent gratitude isn't much use to anyone.

—Gladys B. Stern

23.   If you concentrate on finding what is good in every situation, you will discover that your life will suddenly be filled with gratitude, a feeling that nurtures the soul.

—Rabbi Harold Kushner

24.   Gratitude is not only the greatest of virtues, but the parent of all the others.

—Winston Churchill

25.   The person who has stopped being thankful has fallen asleep in life.

—Robert Louis Stevenson

26. When you are grateful, fear disappears and abundance appears.

—Anthony Robbins

27. What if you gave someone a gift, and they neglected to thank you for it—would you be likely to give them another? Life is the same way. In order to attract more of the blessings that life has to offer, you must truly appreciate what you already have.

—Ralph Marston

28. Find the good—and praise it.

—Alex Haley

29. There is a positive shift emerging in the world today, with more people waking up to the fact that gratitude can make a huge difference to their quality of life and level of happiness.

—Fran Hewitt

30. When a person doesn't have gratitude, something is missing in his or her humanity. A person can almost be defined by his or her attitude toward gratitude.

—Elie Wiesel

A LESSON FROM A STORY

Gratitude unlocks the fullness of life. It turns what we have into enough, and more … Gratitude makes sense of our past, brings peace for today, and creates a vision for tomorrow.

—Melody Beattie

My senior year is drawing to a close. It is the day before my last day of high school, and I can't help but think about the places I have gone, the fantastic people I have met, and the once-in-a-lifetime experiences I have had. Many people and organizations have played key roles in my pursuit of happiness.

First of all, I want to thank my family for always supporting me and believing that I could achieve my wildest dreams. My parents taught me that life isn't fair and that sometimes you will ask yourself if you are actually good enough to reach your goal. But it's not about being number one. It's about learning from each and every experience and growing as a person. They have also shown me the value of becoming a responsible and honest young woman. I have learned that if I want to get respect, I must first give respect.

Next, I want to let my friends know that I appreciate them for putting up with my not-so-average lifestyle as a farm girl. Even though I missed lots of football games and high school dances, they never judged me. I realize how lucky I am to have many true friends. I have been through some of the best and worst times of my life with these individuals, and they were always there for the midnight phone calls and the breakdowns in the school bathroom. You all know who you are, and I truly believe that you all are the greatest blessings a girl could have.

During the last four years, I have undoubtedly lived, breathed, and bled the colors blue and gold! The National FFA Organization has had one of the largest impacts on my life. It has molded me and transformed me to be the leader and agricultural spokesperson I have always wanted to be.

As a freshman I was very quiet and shy, but I wanted to participate in all that FFA had to offer. So I first decided—no, actually, I was tricked by my agriculture teachers—to step out of my comfort zone and participate in the FFA creed speaking contest. I was petrified and felt I wanted to die. However, over the next three years, I conquered my fear and became a two-time state public-speaking finalist and even ran for state FFA officer.

Running for state officer helped me to appreciate all of the leadership skills I have gained. I have become a leader that other FFA members look up to. Although there were many disappointments and challenges along the way, I achieved my dream of becoming the Ohio FFA Star Farmer. Thank you TO and BC for truly changing my life and pushing me beyond what I thought were my limits.

As the largest youth organization in the country, the FFA sponsors many state and national convention and leadership conferences, and I was fortunate to have many opportunities to participate. These experiences truly changed my outlook on life and encouraged me to think about both the decisions I have made and the difference I can truly make in the lives of others. I hadn't given much thought to the impact of a few kind words or a helping hand, until I heard Hannah Crossen, past Ohio FFA President, share a story at a state convention.

Hannah told of a boy who had watched a prank occur as he was walking home from school. The victim was another boy from school, whom he didn't know. Some bullies had passed the boy and purposely knocked a large stack of books from his arms. Feeling compassion for the boy, the observer approached and helped him pick up the books. From that day on, the two boys became best friends, but the story almost had a very tragic ending. You see, the boy was carrying such a large stack of books home because he had cleaned out his locker at school. He was planning to commit suicide, and he didn't want his mother to have to go to school and get his things. That story hit me hard and made me think of the people who have helped save me from giving up on my dreams when I felt that all hope was lost.

Since my first day as a freshman in high school, I have made memories that will last a lifetime. The FFA, my parents, and advisors have all opened countless doors, so that I could explore possibilities for my future. I don't think of these last days of high school as the end of my teenage years, but rather as the beginning of the rest of my life. I am beginning a new journey, but I will never forget my down-home roots and those who helped me get to where I am today.

Lindsey Grimes,
Hillsboro FFA

Who has made a huge impact on your life? Have you expressed your gratitude and appreciation to them?

PERSONAL REFLECTIONS

Write your favorite quote from this chapter in the space below:

_____
_____
_____
_____
_____
_____

Why is this quote especially meaningful to you?

_____
_____
_____
_____
_____
_____
_____

Consider keeping a gratitude journal. What five things would you list for today?

_____
_____
_____
_____
_____
_____
_____

Who deserves to hear words of appreciation from you? What have they done that you are especially thankful for? Practice writing a *gratitude message* below.

_____
_____
_____
_____
_____
_____

Chapter 11

Taking Photos for the Album

Capturing a True Picture of Success

Success is the maximum utilization of the ability that you have.

—Zig Ziglar

Have you ever taken a family vacation that seemed more like a never-ending photo shoot than a much-needed getaway for rest, relaxation, and fun? Our three-week Western vacation was very much a balancing act between the two.

My husband and sons were content to simply experience the vacation, but I, on the other hand, was determined to capture and preserve the memories of our experiences through photographs. I was on a mission to create an album filled with pictures that would show all that we had seen and done.

There were numerous occasions during our trip when I heard groaning from my family, because I insisted that we stop for a photo opportunity. The boys were relieved when I filled the memory card, but their joy was short-lived when I pulled out another card from the camera bag. I went prepared with extra rechargeable batteries too.

It took me weeks to edit and print photos and assemble an album in chronological order, but the entire family has enjoyed the finished product tremendously. Photos are a great way to document any journey, especially your life journey.

You have heard the expression, "A picture is worth a thousand words." If a professional photographer had been tracking your journey since birth, what would the pictures in your album say about you? Where have you gone, and what have you done? What are you doing now? How have you achieved success?

PICTURING SUCCESS

Imagine that you have just been given a blank sheet of paper and a set of markers, along with instructions to draw a picture that illustrates how you have achieved success. What would you draw? Would you draw the grand champion banner you won at the county fair, or would it be a picture of the trophy you won at the regional track meet?

Too many times people equate success with superiority or winning, but achieving success doesn't necessarily mean you have to be *the* best. Success is all about discovering your potential and doing *your* best. So, how are you using your talents and abilities? Do you know what your potential is? Do you give your best effort in all situations?

Reflect for a moment on the following quote by speaker and author John Maxwell. "What does it take to be a success? Two things are required: the right picture of success and the right principles for getting there." Being committed to achieving your goals is one of those fundamental principles. You seldom achieve success overnight.

Do you recognize the names of Kelly Clarkson, Ruben Studdard, Fantasia Barrino, Carrie Underwood, Taylor Hicks, Jordin Sparks, David Cook, and Kris Allen? If you are a fan of *American Idol,* the immensely popular vocal talent reality television series that first aired in 2002, you will recognize the list of names as the winners for the first eight seasons. While the show may seem to launch music careers overnight, the performers will tell you that it has taken years to develop their talent.

For example, consider Carrie Underwood's journey.[1] Carrie grew up singing in church and gradually expanded her audiences to include grade-school musicals and area talent shows. After high school she attended Northeastern State University in Tahlequah, Oklahoma, where she majored in broadcast journalism with her sights set on a career in television news. During the summers, she would perform at the *Downtown Country* show, a Branson-style show that included singing, dancing, and comedy.

It was during her senior year at NSU that she took notice of the news reports concerning tryouts for *American Idol's* 2005 season. Amid the whirlwind of winning *American Idol* in May, Carrie recorded and released her debut album in November of 2005. Despite launching a career in the music industry, she remained committed to her goal of earning a college degree. Carrie completed her studies and graduated magna cum laude in May of 2006.

Distractions, challenges, and even new opportunities can tempt you to take your eye off your goal, but successful individuals recognize the important of commitment over the long haul. What you choose to do day in and day out best demonstrates your commitment.

HABITS DETERMINE YOUR LEVEL OF SUCCESS

Success and failure are both largely the result of habit—the automatic ways you respond and react to what's going on around you. You are where you are and what you are because of your habits. In his book *The Success Principles: How to Get from Where You Are to Where You Want to Be*, author Jack Canfield shares the following:

> Successful people don't just drift to the top. Getting there requires focused action, personal discipline, and lots of energy every day to make things happen. The habits you develop from this day forward will ultimately determine how your future unfolds.[2]

Your daily actions do, indeed, make a huge impact on your ability to achieve success. According to psychologists, up to 90 percent of your actions and reactions are habits.[3] From the time you get up each morning until you go to bed at night, there are hundreds of things you do the same way every day.

Without a change in circumstances or a definite decision on your part to do something differently, you are likely to keep doing the same things indefinitely. You will work in the same job, associate with the same people, eat the same foods, take the same route to school or work, participate in the same recreational activities, and watch the same television shows—unless you consciously decide to make a change.

Habits affect how well every area of your life works—from your job or educational pursuits, to your personal health and wellness, and your relationships with family, friends, and co-workers. Habits can work for you or against you. The choice is yours. Habits are good when they enrich and improve your life. But changes must be made if your habits become major obstacles to achieving success.

CHANGING HABITS

J. Paul Getty, founder of the Getty Oil Company, once said, "The individual who wants to reach the top in *business* must appreciate the might and force of habit. He must be quick to break those habits that can break him—and hasten to adopt those practices that will become the habits that help him achieve the success he desires." Now, reread the quote substituting the word *life* for the word *business*. What a powerful insight!

What habits are hindering your ability to achieve success? Be honest with yourself. Go one step further, and ask others to help you objectively identify what might be holding you back.

Once you have identified a habit that needs to be changed, determine what new behavior will replace it. For example, let's say you are eating fast-food lunches five days a week, and your goal is to reduce the frequency to two or fewer times per week. What will you specifically need to do to change your behavior and create a new habit? Will you start packing a lunch, or will you choose to visit the grocery store and make a salad at the salad bar? What other options do you have? How will you keep a record of the times that you do decide to eat a fast-food lunch? How will you stay motivated? What incentive could you establish that will encourage you to adopt the new habit?

What other bad habits do you need to address? Are you guilty of making sarcastic remarks or poking fun at others? Do you procrastinate and then stay up late to complete a report or research paper? Are you frequently late for appointments? Do you watch too much television? Are you spending more money than you earn? If any of these describe you, now is the time to replace any of these behaviors with more productive habits.

Commit yourself to a new course of action. Your changes could be as fundamental as making your conversations more encouraging and uplifting. Try scheduling time to complete reports and research papers a week prior to their deadlines. Make it a priority to arrive on time for appointments. Read, volunteer, or pursue hobbies instead of watching television. Make purchases with cash, and stop using the credit card.

Identifying and changing the habits that are no longer helping you achieve success can be the hardest things you will ever do. Remember, bad habits are easy to form but hard to live with, while good habits are hard to form but easy to live with.

Don't overwhelm yourself by thinking that new habits are best begun as New Year's resolutions. Instead, pace yourself with the seasons. Identify four habits you need to change or new habits you plan to adopt this year, and commit to working on one each season. The opportunity to achieve success begins each day with a steadfast commitment to developing your new habits.

Don't wait for some external factor to trigger your actions. Rely, instead, on personal initiative, doing what needs to be done without being told. Begin changing your unproductive habits today.

PRACTICE MAKES PERFECT

The good news is that all habits are learned and can, therefore, be unlearned. You can change if you *want* to. Consider using the themes from this book as a guide for selecting and practicing good habits.

- Establish short-term and long-term goals. Have a sense of direction and purpose. Know where you are going.
- Be action oriented. Successful individuals get things done. Don't be afraid of the hard work that is needed to develop your abilities and talents.
- Maintain high standards for personal conduct, and hold true to your values. Understand that excellence is the gradual result of always striving to do better.
- Develop and maintain a positive attitude toward life. When you look for good in others, you will usually find it.
- Think of learning as a joy, not a duty or chore. Continually enrich your life by learning new things and improving yourself.
- Understand that leadership begins with self-mastery. You can't lead others until you can first lead yourself. Take responsibility for your own life instead of blaming others or making excuses.
- Search for ways to be of greater service to others. Sometimes you will be required to put another's needs ahead of your own. True success is the result of doing, not receiving.
- Accept what life brings. Consider difficulties and challenges as opportunities and possibilities. Don't be afraid to explore them.
- Be appreciative and give thanks for what others add to your life. Expressing gratitude helps build good relationships with others.

Do everything within your power to ensure that your habits are stepping stones rather than stumbling blocks. Picture in your mind what success looks like in regard to your personal, family, and professional roles. Identify your potential, and put forth your best effort to achieve success.

SUMMING IT UP

Key points from this chapter include:

- Achieving success doesn't necessarily mean you have to be *the* best. Realizing success is all about discovering your potential and doing *your* best.

- Being committed to achieving your goals is one of the fundamental principles of success. You seldom achieve success overnight.

- Distractions, challenges, and even new opportunities can tempt you to take your eye off your goal, but successful individuals recognize the importance of commitment over the long haul.

- As much as 90 percent of your actions and reactions are habits. What you repeatedly do greatly affects the level of success you can achieve.

- Identifying and changing the habits that are no longer helping you achieve success can be the hardest things you will ever do.

- Research indicates that consistently repeating and reinforcing a new behavior for thirteen weeks can create a positive lifestyle change that will stick with you for life.

- The good news is that all habits are learned and can, therefore, be unlearned. You can change if you *want* to.

Great wisdom can be found in the following words from Norman Vincent Peale: "Formulate and stamp indelibly on your mind a mental picture of yourself as succeeding. Hold this picture tenaciously. Never permit it to fade. Your mind will seek to develop the picture … Do not build up obstacles in your imagination."

WORDS OF WISDOM

1.   Quality is never an accident; it is always the result of high intention, sincere effort, intelligent direction, and skillful execution; it represents the wise choice of many alternatives.

     —Willa A. Foster

2.   Success is not a destination, it is a journey.

     —John Wooden

3.   Your level of performance is a choice. You can settle for mediocrity, or you can strive for excellence. But know this: You can't make adequacy your goal and reach your potential.

     —John Maxwell

4.   Success is not the key to happiness. Happiness is the key to success. If you love what you are doing, you will be successful.

     —Dale Carnegie

5.   Anyone who desires to achieve and become successful must be like a fine craftsman: committed to excellence.

     —John Maxwell

6.   The most important ingredient in the formula of success is knowing how to get along with people.

—Theodore Roosevelt

7.   Personal greatness is not determined by the size of the job but by the size of the effort one puts into the job.

—John Wooden

8.   Life doesn't require that we be the best, only that we try our best.

—H. Jackson Brown, Jr.

9.   A successful person realizes his personal responsibility for self-motivation. He starts with himself, because he possesses the key to his own ignition switch.

—Kemmons Wilson

10.   The price of success is hard work, dedication to the job at hand, and the determination that whether we win or lose, we have applied the best of ourselves to the task at hand.

—Vince Lombardi

11. We are what we repeatedly do. Excellence, then, is not an act but a habit.

    —Aristotle

12. If you are going to achieve excellence in big things, you develop the habit in little matters. Excellence is not an exception, it is a prevailing attitude.

    —Colin Powell

13. Excellence means doing your very best in everything, in every way. That kind of commitment will take you where half-hearted people will never go.

    —John Maxwell

14. If there is any one secret of success, it lies in the ability to get the other person's point of view and see things from that person's angle as well as from your own.

    —Henry Ford

15. Excellence is to do a common thing in an uncommon way.

    —Booker T. Washington

16.   You can become an even more excellent person by constantly setting higher and higher standards for yourself and then by doing everything possible to live up to those standards.

—Brian Tracy

17.   Don't measure yourself by what you have accomplished, but by what you should have accomplished with your ability.

—John Wooden

18.   There are no secrets to success. It is the result of preparation, hard work, and learning from failure.

—Colin Powell

19.   The quality of a person's life is in direct proportion to their commitment to excellence, regardless of their chosen field of endeavor.

—Vincent Lombardi

20.   For most of my life I have believed that success is found in the running of the race. How you run the race—your planning, preparation, practice, and performance—counts for everything. Winning or losing is a by-product, an aftereffect, of that effort.

—John Wooden

21.   The dictionary is the only place that success comes before
       work. Hard work is the price we must pay for success. I think you
       can accomplish anything, if you're willing to pay the price.

                                                        —Vince Lombardi

22.   Put your heart, mind, intellect, and soul even to your smallest
       acts. This is the secret of success.

                                                      —Swami Sivananda

23.   Success is peace of mind, which is a direct result of self-
       satisfaction in knowing you did your best to become the best
       of which you are capable.

                                                         —John Wooden

24.   The will to win, the desire to succeed, the urge to reach your
       full potential … these are the keys that will unlock the door to
       personal excellence.

                                                           —Confucius

25.   There are countless ways of achieving greatness, but any road to
       achieving one's maximum potential must be built on a bedrock
       of respect for the individual, a commitment to excellence, and
       a rejection of mediocrity.

                                                        —Buck Rodgers

26.   A winner is someone who recognizes his God-given talents, works his tail off to develop them into skills, and uses these skills to accomplish his goals.

—Larry Bird

27.   Success means doing the best we can with what we have. Success is in the doing, not the getting—in the trying, not the triumph.

—Wynn Davis

28.   All successful people, men and women, are big dreamers. They imagine what their future could be, ideal in every respect, and then they work every day toward their distant vision, that goal or purpose.

—Brian Tracy

29.   Success is the result of perfection, hard work, learning from failure, loyalty, and persistence.

—Colin Powell

30.   There is a standard higher than merely winning the race: Effort is the ultimate measure of your success.

—John Wooden

A LESSON FROM A STORY

Paint a vivid picture of what you want, and visualize what it will feel like when it becomes a reality. Inspiration will ignite your creativity and passion.

—Fran Hewitt

Being elected as our FFA chapter's news reporter has been a great experience for me. I have always enjoyed taking pictures and scrapbooking, but I never realized exactly how much success was being achieved by those around me. As a news reporter, I began to understand what success was all about. During the year I took hundreds of pictures of the judging teams, the career-development event participants, and of other chapter activities.

Attending the National FFA Convention was a very special experience. It was exciting to see our chapter's American Degree recipients and national proficiency award winners recognized. I was inspired by their accomplishments, and I realized that I also wanted to be on the stage one day. When we take time to notice what others accomplish, we begin to look at our own potential for success in a new way.

During the past year I have learned that success isn't only for those who win first place. Simply doing your best makes you successful. Any award that you win is just icing on the cake. You don't even have to walk across a stage to know deep in your heart that you have given your best effort.

At the State FFA Convention I watched four of my friends receive their State Degrees, and I captured those special moments with my camera. Other members were recognized for proficiency awards. Maybe they received second-place, third-place, or fourth-place awards instead of first, but my pictures captured the pride they felt just to be on that stage. Their being there showed everyone that they were successful in their own way. They had worked hard at doing something that was important to them, and the pride that showed on their faces was an inspiration to all.

I know how they felt. At the state convention, I also got to walk across the stage to receive the gold rating for my chapter reporter's scrapbook. It all started for me because I had pictures of others' success.

Rachel Mullins,
Eastern Brown FFA

What does success look like to you?

PERSONAL REFLECTIONS

Write your favorite quote from this chapter in the space below:

_____
_____
_____
_____
_____
_____

Why is this quote especially meaningful to you?

_____
_____
_____
_____
_____
_____
_____

List three of your good habits that are stepping stones to success:

_____
_____
_____
_____
_____
_____

What habits are stumbling blocks? Identify a habit you will work on changing during the next four seasons.

_____
_____
_____
_____
_____
_____
_____

Chapter 12

Deciding Where to Go from Here

Living with Purpose and Passion

It is good to have an end to journey toward; but it is the journey that matters in the end.

—Ursula K. LeGuin

Your life journey begins at birth and ends when you draw your last breath. The goals you set serve as the compass that guides your direction for a time. But what happens when you achieve a goal and arrive at a destination? You set another goal, and the journey continues.

For some people, unfortunately, the journey is a disconnected series of trips. They arrive at one destination, spend some time there, get restless, and decide to move on. They set a new goal, select a new destination, and strike out on another journey. This disjointed search leaves them unsatisfied. These wanderers are lacking a purpose and a sense of passion.

UNDERSTANDING YOUR PURPOSE

In her book *Knit Together*, author Debbie Macomber writes, "I am absolutely convinced that each of us is created with a God-given purpose. It's what I like to call the *focus* of our lives—the "what" that my life, and yours, is all about."[1]

Think of your purpose as the specific reason, cause, or meaning for your existence. Identifying, acknowledging, and pursuing your purpose is essential for achieving genuine success and fulfillment. Individuals who align their purpose with their profession tend to be the happiest, most successful, and giving people.

Purpose provides meaning and gives direction for the journey. Your purpose is unique to you, and it is shaped by your strengths, personality, and life experiences. Knowing and following your purpose helps you to unlock the doors to opportunity. Purpose is the master key to life and the ultimate compass you need for your journey.

A great book to guide you in understanding your life's purpose was written by Christian author Rick Warren. In his book *The Purpose Driven Life*, Warren suggests that each individual's life purpose comes from God. He writes, "You were made by God and for God—and until you understand that, life will never make sense. It is only in God that we discover our origin, our identity, our meaning, our purpose, our significance, and our destiny. Every other path leads to a dead end."[2]

CREATE A PERSONAL MISSION STATEMENT

Many companies, and even nonprofit organizations, have mission statements. Mission statements provide direction and move an organization in the direction needed to achieve desired outcomes. Mission statements are an enduring statement of purpose. A mission statement explains why a company or organizations does what it does.

Likewise, individuals benefit from developing a personal mission statement for their lives. The act of writing down a mission statement forces you to specifically describe the kind of life you want to live and the contribution you want to make. But a mission statement is more than a list of goals.

Writing a mission statement helps you clarify what you intend to do with your time, energy, resources, and talents. In his book *First Things First*, author Stephen Covey contends that the value of developing a mission statement is found in "*connecting with your own unique purpose and the profound satisfaction that comes from fulfilling it.*"[3]

It will take more than just a few minutes to craft a meaningful mission statement. You will need serious introspection. You may need to rewrite your mission statement several times to make it a true expression of your heart. For some people, it may take several weeks or even months before they feel really comfortable with a mission statement.

If putting your ideas down on paper is a challenge, consider the following questions to help you get started:

What will be at the center of your life? Will your life focus on family, career, having fun, or making money? What role does religious faith play in your life?

What kind of person will you be? What character traits will you strive to have? What are your values? How will you treat other people?

What will you contribute to others? What acts of service will you provide? What difference can you make? What legacy will you leave behind?

I spent several weeks fine-tuning my mission statement. I chose to use my first name as an acronym to define my purpose. My statement reads as follows:

The purpose of my life is to focus on the:
Joy of being a child of God, as I seek
Opportunities to serve others, with
Actions that are encouraging and uplifting, as I work to
Nurture my own mind, body, and spirit.

Not everyone would find the acronym approach a helpful strategy for organizing their thoughts, but the good news is there is no set formula for writing a personal mission statement. Consider these other examples:

I will treasure time spent with my family and friends above everything else, putting aside time for them no matter how busy my schedule may become.

I will strive to make a positive difference in every person I interact with and always continue to improve my body, mind, emotions, and spirit, with truth and love. I will remain teachable and grateful.

I dedicate myself to an attitude of gratitude in order to improve my health and my wealth. With this attitude, I will generously share my time and my talents with my family, my church, and my community.

My purpose is to enhance the lives of those I meet by helping them face demanding and challenging situations with enthusiasm and strength.

I didn't write my mission statement until I was in my late thirties, but I wish I had done so much earlier. The decade of your twenties is a time for searching, testing, and exploring new opportunities. It is a time of change and for becoming more independent. Unfortunately, wanderers often become very frustrated as they struggle with trying to figure out what they want to be when they grow up. Fulfillment seems to be somewhere on the distant horizon of retirement.

The truth, however, is that experiencing fulfillment does not have to be postponed until the golden years. Use your mission statement as the criterion to evaluate every opportunity and decision you make. Knowing your purpose helps you experience significance, regardless of your age. Over time, you will find that your mission statement can change as you grow, learn, and experience life.

DRIVEN BY PASSION

Have you ever questioned why people work? Do you consider work as a necessary means to an end? Many people say they go to work to earn a living. There is nothing fundamentally wrong with that notion, but the risk for burnout is greatest when you can't see beyond the paycheck, or when you don't recognize the greater purpose for the work you do.

President Woodrow Wilson once said, "You are not here merely to make a living. You are here to enable the world to live more amply, with greater vision, and with a finer spirit of hope and achievement. You are here to enrich the world. You impoverish yourself if you forget this errand."

Retired NBC news anchor Tom Brokaw put it another way when he said, "It's easy to make a buck. It's a lot tougher to make a difference." But the essence of significant work is the ability to do both: to earn the money that provides for personal and family needs, while making a difference in the lives of those around you.

When you do what you really enjoy, you contribute to the fulfillment of your mission statement. The passion or emotional energy you bring to your work reduces the likelihood of burnout that tends to haunt those who simply chase after the next paycheck.

Passion cannot be faked for very long, especially with those who know you best. Your passion is evident when you stop doing what others expect you to do and choose to do what you love. Once you know what you are passionate about doing—do it! Pursue it, regardless of the financial benefits or consequences. As the popular sayings go, "Do what you love, and the money will follow. Do what you love, and you will never have to work a day in your life."

BEGIN WITH THE END IN MIND

Stephen Covey, author of the best-selling book *The 7 Habits of Highly Effective People*, challenges his readers to *begin with the end in mind*. He is referring to living your life with a clear understanding of your final destination. It means you should know where you are now, so that you can make the decisions and take the necessary actions to move you to where you want to be.

Unfortunately, many people find it very easy to get caught up in the rat race of life. Covey offers the following warning, "It's incredibly easy to get caught up in an activity trap, in the *busyness* of life, to work harder and harder at climbing the ladder of success only to discover it's leaning against the wrong wall. It is possible to be busy—very busy—without being very effective."[4]

Is your ladder leaning against the right wall? Choose to use your mission statement as a road map, and let your passion be the fuel. When you do, each day can be a source of joy and fulfillment.

A PURPOSE BRINGS YOUR JOURNEY FULL CIRCLE

Writing this book has indeed been a rewarding personal journey for me. The twelve themes presented in the book have been frequently tested during the two years it has taken me to research, organize quotations, write, and publish this book. I have been challenged to:

- Set goals
- Use values as the rules to guide me
- Plan and take action
- Monitor my own self-talk and attitude
- Lead myself
- Take time to learn and grow
- Find opportunities to volunteer
- Overcome challenges
- Hang tough with perseverance
- Express gratitude and appreciation
- Keep a true picture of success in my mind
- Live with purpose and passion

The writing of this book has positively affected my efforts to fulfill my personal mission statement. Let me show you how. As stated earlier, *the purpose of my life is to focus on the*:

- ❖ *Joy of being a child of God.* Throughout this book I have included scripture references as well as a story illustration from the Bible. I have been forthright in declaring that my Christian faith is important to me, but I believe that the insights shared from the selected examples are valuable regardless of the reader's religious affiliation or lack thereof.
- ❖ *Opportunities to serve others.* I remained steadfast in my belief that teens and young adults could benefit greatly from a positive message that guides their life journey and helps them realize personal fulfillment.
- ❖ *Actions that are encouraging and uplifting.* Words can definitely be empowering and encouraging. It was my desire that this book be a positive resource for personal reflection.
- ❖ *Nurturing my own mind, body, and spirit.* Stepping out of my comfort zone and taking on the new endeavor of writing a book certainly required a commitment to learning new things, pushing myself physically, and testing my faith. Had I overlooked any of the three during the two-year process I would have probably been unsuccessful.

"So, now what?" you may be asking. I have come full circle, and it's back to chapter 1 for me, as I work to set my next *SMART* goal. Let the journey continue for you, as well. As suggested in the *About this Book* section, begin again on the first day of next month to reread and reflect on one quotation each day. You will have a year's worth of positive insight to keep your journey on track.

A SPECIAL INVITATION

Rereading and reflecting on the quotations can provide you with very powerful "aha!" moments. An insightful statement might prompt you to say, "Oh, I so agree with that statement because …" and your own personal story or example might spill out.

I am very appreciative of the student leaders and FFA alumni who have contributed the personal stories featured at the end of each chapter. As a high-school or college student, you have likewise had numerous experiences that support many of the fundamental principles included in this book. What connections were you able to make between the quotes and your own personal experiences? Which quotes gave you the best "aha!" moments?

As a follow-up project, I plan to compile and publish a collection of stories written by young adults. I invite you to select a quote that strikes a chord with you and then write your own personal story. Feel free to use the stories included in this book as a guide.

Please include your personal contact information (name, year of high-school graduation, address, e-mail address, and name of youth organization that has had the biggest impact on you) along with your story, and send your contribution to me via mail or e-mail:

MAIL
Joan Garrett
9701 Cherry Fork Rd.
Winchester, OH 45697

E-MAIL
thoughtsforjoan@yahoo.com

I look forward to reading a story about your personal journey.

SUMMING IT UP

Key points from this chapter include:

- Identifying, acknowledging, and pursuing your purpose is essential for achieving genuine success and fulfillment.

- Knowing and following your purpose helps you unlock doors of opportunity. Purpose is the master key to life.

- Writing and following your mission statement helps you to clarify what you intend to do with your time, energy, resources, and talents.

- You do not have to postpone experiencing fulfillment until the golden years. Knowing your purpose helps you experience significance, regardless of your age.

- The risk for burn-out is highest when you can't see beyond the next paycheck or when you don't recognize the greater purpose for the work you do.

- Once you know what you are passionate about doing—do it! Pursue it regardless of the financial benefits or consequences.

- "Begin with the end in mind" means to live your life with a clear understanding of your final destination.

As a general rule, more people regret things they *didn't* do than things they *did* do. There is a long-term price to pay for not following your heart.

WORDS OF WISDOM

1. Take the blueprint of who you are, with your gifts, unique talents, and personality, and align them with the passion of your spirit. This is the foundation for your purpose.

    —Fran Hewitt

2. Where your talents and the needs of the world cross, your calling can be found.

    —Aristotle

3. Each of us has a purpose for which we were created. Our responsibility—and our greatest joy—is to identify it.

    —John Maxwell

4. The whole secret of a successful life is to find out what it is one's destiny to do, and then do it.

    —Henry Ford

5. We were created for purpose. To be intentional. To move. To focus our actions and our abilities for a specific reason.

    —Debbie Macomber

6. Each and every one of us should have something we're chasing every single morning, to be excited about the day, and then go after it.

—Kevin Carroll

7. We must have a theme, a goal, a purpose in our lives. If you don't know where you're aiming, you don't have a goal. My goal is to live my life in such a way that when I die, someone can say, she cared.

—Mary Kay Ash

8. Without a clear purpose, you have no foundation on which you base decisions, allocate your time, and use your resources.

—Rick Warren

9. A true measure of your worth includes all the benefits others have gained from your success.

—Cullen Hightower

10. What we are is God's gift to us. What we become is our gift to God.

—Frances Hyatt

11.   Without a purpose, life is motion without meaning, activity without direction, and events without reason. Without a purpose, life is trivial, petty, and pointless.

—Rick Warren

12.   Many people have a wrong idea of what constitutes true happiness. It is not attained through self-gratification, but through fidelity to a worthy purpose.

—Helen Keller

13.   Winners are people with definite purpose in life.

—Denis Waitley

14.   I think the purpose of life is to be useful, to be responsible, to be honorable, to be compassionate. It is, after all, to matter: to count, to stand for something, to have made some difference that you lived at all.

—Leo C. Rosten

15.   The greatest use of a life is to spend it on something that will outlast it.

—William James

16. Without knowing what I am and why I am here, life is impossible.

—Leo Tolstoy

17. A big part of life is figuring out what your gifts are and how you are supposed to use them. When this happens, you can expect a positive surge of energy, like a butterfly shedding its cocoon and preparing to fly.

—Fran Hewitt

18. Efforts and courage are not enough without purpose and direction.

—John F. Kennedy

19. We have made a least a start in discovering the meaning in human life when we plant shade trees under which we know full well we will never sit.

D. Elton Trueblood

20. You can't follow your dreams if you don't understand your purpose, and you can't take risks if you aren't passionate about your dreams.

—Debbie Macomber

21. No man or woman is an island. To exist just for yourself is meaningless. You can achieve the most satisfaction when you feel related to some greater purpose in life, something greater than yourself.

—Denis Waitley

22. Make your life a mission—not an intermission.

—Arnold H. Glasgow

23. Purpose defines our contribution to life. It may find expression through family, community, relationship, work, and spiritual activities. We receive from life what we give, and in the process we understand more of what it means to discover our purpose.

Richard J. Leider

24. People's purpose in life is always connected to their giftedness.

—John Maxwell

25. A successful life is one that is lived through understanding and pursuing one's own path, not chasing after the dreams of others.

—Chin-Ning Chu

26. If you want your life to have impact, focus it! Stop dabbling. Stop trying to do it all. Do less. Prune away even good activities and do only that which matters most.

—Rick Warren

27. Life isn't about finding yourself. Life is about creating yourself.

—George Bernard Shaw

28. When you heed the calling of your heart, you are following your purpose. Having purpose in your life gives you the courage to do the things you are meant to do.

—Rhonda Britten

29. The cost of living abundantly is that you must get out all that lies within you and become the person that you have always wanted to be, not only for yourself but also for the benefit of others in this world.

—Delatorro McNeal II

30. You can't follow your dreams if you don't understand your purpose, and you can't take risks if you aren't passionate about your dreams.

—Debbie Macomber

A LESSON FROM A STORY

Every journey has to start somewhere, and believing in yourself is the first step toward achieving your purpose.

—Debbie Macomber

I have been an active member of my FFA chapter for all four years of high school, but I had a slow start. I was just like a lot of other freshmen, in that I was scared of the seniors and lacked in confidence. I tried to blend in with the crowd, but I realized I wasn't being the person I wanted to be. I had skills just waiting to be developed, but I didn't know how to do it. I turned to my mom for advice.

My mom had also been a four-year member of the Eastern Brown FFA chapter, except she was outgoing from the beginning. She had served as an officer for three years, participated in many activities, and had the full FFA experience. When I went to her with my concerns, she said she noticed I had been acting differently since I had started high school.

My enthusiasm must have been evident that first day of school, when I came home and told her, "I found my people!" She thought that since I had so much fun on my first day I would soon start developing my skills and talent right away, but she didn't realize that I was afraid to stand out. I was afraid of failing at whatever I did. This agriculture (ag) experience was completely new to me, and I didn't know what aspect would be my forte. Mom suggested that I talk to my ag instructors.

I took her advice and told my instructors that I wanted to participate in different activities, but I didn't know what I would be good at. I told them to expect very little from me, since I had no idea what I was doing or how to do it. That gave them a good laugh, but I sure didn't see anything humorous about not knowing what to do. They signed me up for everything I could possibly do in my first year of ag. I participated in public speaking, but I really didn't enjoy it that much, so I tried other activities.

When I was elected to an officer position, I knew I had finally found my niche. I loved being a leader. I finally began to experience the satisfaction that comes from using and developing my innate skills for leading others. I had found my purpose for being in FFA. I had found the one thing that I could do best—lead a group of people.

After realizing where my greatest talent could be used, I stretched my ability as far as I could. I gained the confidence to apply my public-speaking skills toward benefiting an entire chapter instead of just myself. Under my leadership, the second-year members organized and conducted kindergarten ag day, a field day that teaches five-year-olds how American agriculture provides our food supply. As chapter historian, I assisted the reporter in creating our official scrapbook, and as chapter treasurer I was responsible for our chapter's finances. It was an honor to be elected as president of our chapter for my senior year.

As a graduating senior, it is difficult to leave behind an outstanding youth organization. The chapter has been my extended family. Many of my best friends have also been members, and I have had great mentors thanks to my involvement in the FFA. They have helped me realize an important purpose for life and see my true potential as a leader. I look forward to the new leadership opportunities that will come my way in college and beyond.

Candice Yockey,
Eastern Brown FFA

**What excites you? How can your passion lead
to personal and professional fulfillment?**

PERSONAL REFLECTIONS

Write your favorite quote from this chapter in the space below:

_____
_____
_____
_____
_____
_____
_____
_____

Why is this quote especially meaningful to you?

_____
_____
_____
_____
_____
_____
_____
_____

Begin to draft a personal mission statement in the space provided below:

_____
_____
_____
_____
_____
_____

What are you passionate about? How do your current job or future career plans enable you to pursue your passion?

_____
_____
_____
_____
_____
_____

Notes

About this Book

1. Jim Tressel, *The Winners Manual for the Game of Life.* (Carol Stream, IL: Tyndale House, 2008), 8–10.

Chapter 3

1. Driving directions, MapQuest, http://www.mapquest.com (accessed March 6, 2009).

2. John C. Maxwell, *Your Road Map for Success: You Can Get There from Here.* (Nashville, TN: Thomas Nelson, Inc., 2002), 80.

3. Jack Canfield, *The Success Principles: How to Get from Where You are to Where You Want to Be* (New York, NY: HarperCollins, 2005), 99.

Chapter 4

1. James Allen, *As a Man Thinketh.* (New York, NY: Barnes & Noble, 2007; originally published in 1902), 9.

2. John C. Maxwell, *Your Road Map for Success: You Can Get There from Here.* (Nashville, TN: Thomas Nelson, Inc., 2002), 50.

3. Ibid., 65.

Chapter 5

1. Mark Sanborn, *You Don't Need a Title to Be a Leader.* (New York, NY: Doubleday, 2006), 8.

2. John C. Maxwell, *The 360° Leader: Developing Your Influence from Anywhere in the Organization* (Nashville, TN: Thomas Nelson, Inc., 2005), 7.

3. Mark Sanborn, *You Don't Need a Title to be a Leader* (New York, NY: Doubleday, 2006), 31.

Chapter 6

1. Stephen Covey, *The 7 Habits of Highly Effective People* (New York, NY: Fireside, 1989), 287.

2. Tom Rath, *Strengths Finder 2.0* (New York, NY: Gallup Press, 2007).

3. Dondi Scumaci, *Designed for Success* (Lake Mary, FL: Excel Books, 2008), 183.

Chapter 7

1. Our Role and Impact, Corporation for National and Community Service, http://www.nationalservice.gov/about/role _ impact/index.asp (accessed March 13, 2009).

2. What is Service Learning? National Service-Learning Corporation, http://www.servicelearning.org/what-service-learning (accessed March 13, 2009).

Chapter 9

1. *Webster's Pocket Dictionary and Thesaurus* (Reisterstown, MD: Nichols, 1999), 190.

2. Dig a Little Deeper, Afterhours Inspirational Stories, http:// www.inspirationalstories.com/cgi-bin/printer.pl?881 (accessed November 17, 2009).

Chapter 10

1. Dr. Robert Emmons on Gratitude, First 30 Days, http://www. first30days.com/experts/dr-robert-emmons (accessed September 18, 2009).

2. I-Messages, Only-Effective-Communication-Skills, http://www. only-effective-communication-skills.com/imessages.html (accessed September 12, 2009).

Chapter 11

1. Biography, The Official Carrie Underwood Site, http://www. carrieunderwoodofficial.com/biography (accessed August 15, 2009).

2. Jack Canfield, *The Success Principles: How to Get from Where You are to Where You Want to Be* (New York, NY: HarperCollins, 2005), 248.

3. Ibid., 247.

Chapter 12

1. Debbie Macomber, *Knit Together: Discover God's Pattern for Your Life* (New York, NY: FaithWords, 2007), 5.

2. Rick Warren, *The Purpose Driven Life* (Grand Rapids, Michigan: Zondervan, 2002), 18.

3. Stephen R. Covey with A. Roger Merrill and Rebecca R. Merrill, *First Things First* (New York, NY: Fireside, 1995), 107.

4. Stephen R. Covey, *The 7 Habits of Highly Effective People* (New York, NY: Fireside, 1989), 97–98.

Acknowledgments

Thus I set to paper with delight.
And quickly had my thoughts in black and white.
For having now my method by the end,
Still as I pulled, it came; and so I penned.

—John Bunyan, *The Pilgrim's Progress*

If only it could be so easy to write a book! The "penning" of it is only the beginning of a long process that involves many people, whom I eagerly take this opportunity to thank. My appreciation goes far beyond what the words written here can express.

My family, Brian, Clay, and Jacob: Thank you for supporting and encouraging this project.

My parents, Charles and Nancy Grimes: Thank you for encouraging and supporting my involvement in youth organizations while I was in high school. I also appreciate your willingness to assist with editing my manuscript.

Ohio FFA Executive Secretary Steve Gratz: Thank you for including information about this book project on the Ohio FFA Web site.

FFA advisors Sarah Lucha, Jessica Tracey, Libby French, Gigi Neal, and Luke Rhonemus: I greatly appreciate the opportunity to meet with your students and collect their stories. I would also like to thank Jaime Chenevey for submitting her students' stories by mail.

FFA members: A special thanks to all the FFA members who shared their personal stories for possible inclusion in this book.

Author Mark Sanborn: Thank you for providing the foreword for this book. As a former National FFA President, you understood my vision.

My friends Rebecca Parker and Bronwyn Jones: I greatly appreciate the time you spent reviewing my manuscript.

Publisher iUniverse: Thank you for providing professional editing services, for designing the book's cover, and for leading me through the publishing process.